QUIET MIRACLES
A True Story of Love and Courage

Brenton G. Yorgason

with illustrations by Aaron Yorgason

Covenant Communications, Inc.

Covenant Communications, Inc.
American Fork. Utah

Printed in the United States of America
First Printing: May 1994
94 95 96 97   10 9 8 7 6 5 4 3 2 1

Quiet Miracles
ISBN 1-55503-691-0

Books authored and/or co-authored by Brenton G. Yorgason

QUIET MIRACLES: A True Story of Love and Courage
STANDING TALL: The Shawn Bradley Story
Simeon's Touch
The Garrity Test
TY: The Ty Detmer Story
NAMINA—Biography of Georganna Bushman Spurlock (private printing)
Six Secrets of Self Renewal and Relationship Enhancement
The First Christmas Gift
Prayers on the Wind
Spiritual Survival in the Last Days
Here Stands a Man
Roger and Sybil Ferguson History (private printing)
Little Known Evidences of the Book of Mormon
Sacred Intimacy
Receiving Answers to Prayer
Obtaining the Blessings of Heaven
Pardners: Three Stories on Friendship
In Search of Steenie Bergman (Soderberg Series #5)
KING—The Life of Jerome Palmer King (private printing)
The Greatest Quest
Seven Days for Ruby (Soderberg Series #4)
Dirty Socks and Shining Armor—A Tale from King Arthur's Camelot
The Eleven-Dollar Surgery
Becoming
Tales From the Book of Mormon
Brother Brigham's Gold (Soderberg Series #3)
Ride the Laughing Wind
The Miracle
The Thanksgiving Promise (Made into Disney Classic TV Movie)
Chester, I Love You (Soderberg Series #2)
Double Exposure
Seeker of the Gentle Heart
The Krystal Promise
A Town Called Charity, and Other Stories about Decisions
The Bishop's Horse Race (Soderberg Series #1)
Windwalker (Movie Version—Out of Print)
Others
From First Date to Chosen Mate
From Two to One (Out of Print)
From This Day Forth (Out of Print)
Creating a Celestial Marriage (textbook)
Marriage and Family Stewardships (textbook)

TO REQUEST ORDER FORM, CONTACT:

The Brent Yorgason Company
3962 E Alpine Valley Circle
Sandy, Utah 84092
Phone 801-943-6745

CONTENTS

PART ONE

THE REFINER'S FIRE

Prophets, both ancient and modern, have taught that Jesus Christ is the REFINER. His mission is to purify, cleanse, and ultimately refine the human soul so that the children of men may return to His Kingdom. Byron and Caryl Mackay, at a very early age, began to experience this "fire," and both of them responded in a marvelous, exemplary manner.

PROLOGUE

Byron Smith Mackay was born in Granger, Utah, on the 17th day of January, 1930. His early years were spent in perfect health. When he reached the age of 12, however, he was stricken with rheumatic fever. He had just received the Aaronic Priesthood, and it was very disturbing that he was too ill to enjoy the life that was his. Although he eventually recovered, it would be years before he understood the lasting effects of this illness.

At age 17, Byron married Caryl Nielson in the Salt Lake L.D.S. Temple, thus forming a union that will assuredly extend into the eternities. However, life was not to be an easy road for Byron and Caryl to follow. When Byron neared his twentieth birthday, many dreams ended, as he was stricken with rheumatoid arthritis. This condition not only drained all of his energy, but his muscles began to contract, leaving him badly crippled. Within months, his weight dropped from 175 to 109 pounds, and he found himself knocking on death's door.

Through faith, prayer, and courage, quiet miracles were wrought, and Byron and Caryl began a most extraordinary journey that spanned the next four decades. Finally, on January 26, 1992, just nine days after celebrating his 62nd birthday, Byron quietly closed his eyes and left this world.

The pages that follow reveal a tender story of love and courage, taken from several volumes of journals that Byron (even with his crippled hands) and his wife, Caryl, religiously kept. In addition, extensive interviews with Caryl, and with Ned Winder, a close personal friend, have yielded as accurate an account as possible, as events were remembered and conversations were reflected upon.

As Caryl related her story to me, I found myself yearning to know more of this remarkable woman and her husband, Byron. In the pages that follow, it is my hope that you will

be edified and enlightened, as this couple's life casts its light like a powerful beacon. At Caryl's request, Byron's favorite scriptures are included at the beginning of each chapter.
  Brenton G. Yorgason

• ONE •
NEAR DEATH'S DOOR

*And again, it shall come to pass that he that hath faith in me
to be healed, and is not appointed unto death, shall be healed.
D&C 42:48*

The Middle of February, 1952

Beads of perspiration formed on Byron's forehead, and
his eyes squinted, as he struggled to shield his eyes from the
bright overhead light. Grimacing in pain, he attempted to
adjust his position, knowing that what he really needed was
a nurse to assist him. Why, if only—

"Good morning, Byron. Are you feeling better this
morning?"

As if by answer to an unspoken prayer, Byron looked up
to see a nurse standing over him, a needle and gauze in her
hand.

"I really wish I was, ma'am. For a 22-year-old guy who's
used to loading several hundred gallons of milk into a truck
every day, I don't even have the strength to lift my arms off
the bed."

Silently, then, and without answering, the nurse turned

him onto his side, administered another pain-killing injection, and exited.

Again, Byron was alone. Alone and very frightened! Even though earlier that morning they had wheeled another patient into his room, still Byron felt totally alone. It was as though his entire life was hung suspended over a gaping hole as vast as the Grand Canyon, waiting to drop into oblivion.

As Byron gazed out the window, his thoughts turned to winter. Large glistening snowflakes fell silently toward the ground, reflecting the rays of the early morning sun that peeked inexplicably through the eastern clouds. The automobiles below were inching their way northward along State Street, coming into the city from as far away as Midvale and Murray. The Salt Lake County Hospital, where he lay, on the corner of 21st South and State, seemed to Byron to be a world away. After all, his world—all twenty-one years of it—had been spent in the outlying farm community of Granger.

At that moment, Byron's thoughts turned to his wife, Caryl. Theirs had been a perfect temple union, and yet now, after just three years of marriage, he was lying helplessly in a hospital bed, unable to move! It wasn't fair—certainly not what he would expect God to allow! In fact, the more Byron's thoughts turned to his pain and near paralysis, the more anger he felt toward God! Why, what if all he had been taught regarding the Restoration and the Book of Mormon was all a total farce?! After all, hadn't he been taught that God was fair and just, and that He was kind and loving toward His children? Well, Byron reasoned, there was nothing fair or just or loving about this!

Sure . . . he had received priesthood blessings over the past year, several of them. Yet now, as his wife and his mother pressed for him to receive another blessing, Byron simply could not bring himself to do it. What good did it do him, anyway? After all, the blessings only increased his anxiety and anger. Instead of getting better, he merely continued to decline in health, until at last he was left to die, probably right here in the hospital.

As these thoughts tumbled in his mind, Byron reasoned that there might not even be a God, let alone one who cared. But if that was true, then who was he angry with? Things just didn't make sense. If he did die, which he honestly felt he would, and if there was a God, then he would come face to face with Him. If that happened, what was he to say to Him?

As these questions passed again and again through his mind, Byron felt his spirits sink even lower. He would never again be able to work, to provide for Caryl and their precious children. His mind wandered, then, to memories of his career at the dairy. He had worked at Winder Dairy since entering high school, loading milk onto the delivery trucks early in the mornings. Co-workers often commented on his unusual physical strength, and he was widely admired for the muscles that rippled along his upper torso. Because of this attention, and because he understood the value of physical conditioning, staying in shape had become almost a passion for him. Even after he had been promoted to a job inside the bottling plant, he made sure that his work was rigorous enough that he remained in robust athletic condition.

As he twisted again in excruciating pain, Byron's thoughts switched to his two-year-old son, Glen. According to Byron's mother, Glen was a mirror image of him, two decades earlier, when he was a toddler. Glen was walking now and making perfect sense with the entertaining sentences he constructed. And of course there was his new baby daughter, Peggy, who had been born the previous September. Like her mother, she was beautiful, and would become a delightful playmate for Glen. But that all hurt to remember, as Byron felt with near certainty that he wouldn't even live to enjoy his children again.

Byron's physical pain had begun a year earlier, when he had felt soreness in his joints. Under the direction of his family physician, Dr. John Ball, he had gone to several chiropractors, thinking that they would find the key to his problem and that in no time he would be well. He had even tried health foods and an electric shock treatment, but to no avail. Now, as he lay in the hospital crippled with confirmed rheumatoid arthritis, he felt his very life slipping away, and there was nothing he could do to stop it.

Byron's boss, George Winder, had always spoken so positively about Byron's illness, assuring him that it was just a temporary setback. But that had been in April, when George recognized Byron's increased limitations and had literally created a job for Byron, as night watchman. The dairy had never used a watchman before that; but with Byron needing help to even walk, it was really the only thing he could do. Then, the day after Peggy was born, he had been fitted with crutches, upon which he became totally dependent to get around.

Byron's night watchman's shift lasted from 4:00 P.M. until 1:00 A.M. He remembered the total frustration and embarrassment he felt each night, upon returning home, as it would take Caryl at least 20 minutes to help him from the car into the house. But now that, too, was gone! He had been forced to quit on December 18, and now, just months later, he was little more than a helpless, nearly paralyzed burden. What made matters even worse was that his mind could still think and reason—and experience the anger and helplessness that was consuming him!

"Hello, young man," a voice suddenly spoke, jarring Byron's thoughts back to the present. "How was your night?"

Glancing up out of the corner of his eye, Byron could see

Dr. Samuelson, the specialist, leaning over him. He was wearing a starched, white uniform, and was smiling.

"Oh . . . hi, doc. I didn't see you come in."

"Hope I didn't awaken you, Byron. Did you sleep okay last night?"

"I'd be a liar if I said I did," Byron grimaced, not wanting to show the pain he was in. "But, Avril over there, has been snoring quite peacefully . . . so at least one of us is enjoying himself."

At that moment, Avril, who was a welfare patient, opened his eyes and spoke.

"Morning, doc. . ."

"Good morning to you, sir."

"Doc, could I please get hooked up to that pain killer stuff that's dripping into Byron's veins?"

"Of course," the doctor quietly replied. "It's called A.C.T.H. The nurses should be bringing it to you any time now.

"But gentlemen," he continued, pulling up a chair and situating himself so that he could speak to both of them, "I must be very honest with you and let you know where you stand. Actually, both of you are in the difficult, advanced stages of rheumatoid arthritis. I have, of course, told you this before. The good news is that, barring some unforseen problem, you should both live for many years."

"What's the bad news, doc?" Byron pressed, sensing that a bomb was about to drop.

"The bad news, Byron, is that both of you must be fitted for body casts. You have the choice of being in either a sitting or standing position when the cast is fitted. But remember, whichever you choose, you will have to assume that position for the rest of your life."

"But doctor," the man Avril protested, "I can't possibly afford to—"

"I've already visited with the state officials, Avril, and

your expenses are fully covered. But, back to your choices. The standing cast, of course, does not mean that you will be standing for the rest of your life. It just means that you will be stretched out in bed, rather than curled up. If you choose the sitting cast, then you can more easily get around, using a wheelchair during the daylight hours. This would be my personal preference."

Byron was stunned! His mind simply could not grasp the fact that he would become permanently cast into a given position—losing all of his mobility for life!

"I felt," Dr. Samuelson continued, "that you deserved to learn of this privately. You are free to share it with your families, of course. I must be going, but I will be happy to visit with you, and with them, as questions arise. Now, please excuse me, as I am late for surgery."

With those words ringing in the air, the busy doctor left the room, allowing the burden of his revelation to settle heavily upon the two men. The specialist's reasoning was clear; the two could talk between themselves and reach a conclusion without his having to spend further time with them.

But the men didn't talk. Instead, each slipped into his own world, trying to comprehend the consequences of the dreadful choice before him. The sitting cast would restrict the wearer from ever stretching out his limbs, either to stand up or to lie down. The standing body cast, on the other hand, would prohibit ever sitting again, either for a meal or for daily use of chairs, sofas, automobile travel, etc.

As the man named Avril considered his options, he was quite sure that he would choose the sitting body cast, so that he could at least spend the rest of his life in a somewhat mobile posture. Byron, for his part, didn't really think it mattered. He wasn't going to live, anyway. Pain kept him from grasping the possibility of having any kind of cast put on him. How could he stand to be even more imprisoned?

That evening Caryl arrived at the hospital, and Byron rehearsed with her the options Dr. Samuelson had prescribed. As the facts were presented, Caryl experienced an overwhelming feeling that Byron should not accept a body cast of any sort. Later, she visited with Dr. Samuelson and was able to share her impressions, as well as to vent her frustrations regarding the lack of attention Byron had received in the hospital to that point. Dr. Samuelson was surprised at her response and indicated that it was his impression that they were uninsured, and so there was little that could be done. But Caryl assured him that they were insured through their employment at Winder Dairy, and that although it was just a minor policy, they would scrape together whatever additional funds needed to get Byron better. After all, she knew that her marriage to Byron was founded upon the principles of faith and obedience, and furthermore, because they had paid an honorable tithe, she felt assured that they would have the ability to meet this financial obligation.

Later that night, as his roommate slept with evident soundness, Byron lay awake in increasing pain. He found himself wishing for death to take him—sensing that this was the only way the pain would cease.

Then, as he learned that two elders from the Church were visiting in the hospital, Byron suddenly perceived that his false pride and lack of faith had been preventing him from receiving further blessings. And so, with feelings born of desperation and forced humility, Byron asked for, and received, a priesthood blessing. At last, though still reeling in physical pain, Byron surrendered to an inner peace with the new knowledge that his life was now in the Lord's hands.

And so, as the night wore on, Byron felt loved by the Lord, even though his body limbs were still throbbing. At the moment of total despair, when he knew he could endure no more, something strange and totally unexpected happened. One instant he was racked with pain, praying that God would allow him to die, and the next, he felt lighter than air, with no sensation of pain. Almost floating in air, Byron sensed that there were others around his bedside—deceased family members who had been permitted to minister to his needs, and perhaps even accept him as he passed into the world of spirits.

At that moment, Byron saw and felt the beauty and joys of the Spirit World, and he found himself unafraid of dying. Instead, he longed to have these feelings continue and to savor the newness of this pain-free existence.

At last, after what seemed hours, Byron opened his eyes and found to his surprise that he was still lying in the hospital bed—very much alive, but free from pain. He understood, then, that he had been given a sacred knowledge, which would provide a foundation of faith and assurance in his life. This experience would give him the strength to spend his days, and his years, in service to his God. A great blanket of warmth enveloped him, allowing his entire frame to relax and welcome the relief.

Quietly then, with deep reverence and gratitude, Byron closed his eyes a second time and wept. He then offered up a silent prayer of thanksgiving. He knew that he and his beautiful sweetheart, Caryl, would rear their children in righteousness, and one day return and dwell with God. He would be given strength from above. Somehow, in the wonders of the heavens, he would be given the means to provide for his family . . . and at least occasionally experience relief from physical pain.

With these thoughts tumbling through his mind, Byron smiled, breathed deeply, and immediately escaped into the peaceful, inviting world of sleep.

• TWO •
A NEW BEGINNING

Choose you this day whom ye will serve . . . but as for me and my house, we will serve the Lord. Joshua 24:15

Following a night of pain-free, restful sleep, Byron awakened with a start. As his eyes focused on the window ahead, he realized that he was still confined to a hospital bed. But, on this morning, something was different—somehow it was not the same.

At that moment, Byron's mind grasped the fact that he felt less pain than he had in months! Glancing up, he could see the bottle of A.C.T.H., or cortisone, as it hung suspended above him, with its serum dripping directly into his veins. He remembered, then, the priesthood blessing he had received during the night, and marveled that his body was responding so immediately to that which had been promised.

A flood of memories from years past came to him of priesthood power at work. He felt badly that he had ever allowed doubts to consume his energies in the past.

A tear formed in the corner of his eye, slid down his face and onto his pillow. He felt bathed in an ocean of gratitude and realized that he had a new sense of appreciation for the very blessing of life itself. More than ever before, he understood how miracles had been wrought.

A mental picture formed in his head, as if on a movie screen, and his mind seemed to travel back in time, to the moment his family had first tasted the fruits of the restoration. The year was 1840, just ten years after the Church had been restored. His great grandfather, Thomas Mackay, had emigrated from Ireland to the Isle of Man. He had married Ann Rodgers, ten years his senior, who loved him dearly.

Not long after their marriage, Thomas and Ann met a Mormon missionary, Elder John Taylor. Elder Taylor was a newly ordained apostle, and had just come to England as a missionary. He had traveled to the Isle of Man to visit the birthplace of his wife and while there taught Thomas and Ann the restored truths of the gospel. They were converted and baptized, and before long found themselves sailing to America, to join with the body of the Church in Nauvoo.

Byron marveled as he considered the friendship that Thomas and Ann shared with the Prophet Joseph Smith and his wife, Emma. And to think that Thomas worked full-time as a carpenter and mason on the Nauvoo Temple! From the record Thomas kept, Byron knew that it gave him great joy to attend the "School of the Prophets." This school instructed worthy adult male members of the Church in the doctrines of the kingdom, with the object of preparing them to proclaim the gospel to the world.

Three years later, just 10 months after Joseph and Hyrum were martyred, Thomas received his patriarchal blessing under the hands of Patriarch John Smith. In this blessing, he had been instructed to return to his native land and to proclaim the gospel to his family. This he had obediently done, after which he journeyed with his wife to Zion, the land of the Great Salt Lake. They entered the valley with Brigham Young and the other initial party of Saints together, and then spent their first winter in the old Salt Lake Fort.

When spring of 1848 finally arrived, Thomas and Ann homesteaded a piece of land south of the platted 40 acres of Temple Square. After planting their first crop, they witnessed the converging of the black blanket of crickets and the miracle of the gulls. When this near disaster was averted, they found only a small portion of grain remaining. Thus, they were rationed two ounces of flour a day for several weeks, with whatever wild roots they could find as a supplement. Primarily they dug seagull roots and gathered thistle tops, which they cooked for greens to round out their diet. They also cooked the tanned hides of animals to create a broth from which they would sustain life. Living this next year in a dugout near the Jordan River, they understood fully the meaning of deprivation and survival.

As Byron considered the sacrifices of his great grandfather Mackay, he knew that this man had experienced trials that he would never even understand.

And what about his grandfather, Manasseh Smith, on his mother's side? He had likewise been born in England, in 1853, and together with his bride, Mary Ann, had joined the Church in spite of the persecution that was heaped upon them. They had then journeyed to America, traveling across the plains and settling first in Murray and then in Granger.

Byron smiled as he thought of Manasseh and Mary Ann's eleven children. How did they keep their sanity? With just two children, he was in overload as a father! The amazing thing, to Byron, was that after the birth of Manasseh's last child, he had been called on a mission to England. The very day that his eighteen-year-old son, Willy, drove him to the train station in the horse and buggy, Willy caught pneumonia. In fact, the first letter Manasseh received from his Mary Ann contained the tragic announcement of Willy's death. Six months later their fifth child, a blossoming early teenager named Harriet, became suddenly ill and died. Byron remembered reading Mary Ann's words, "Father must not come home." And Manasseh didn't come home, but continued to serve faithfully until his mission was completed.

Like Thomas Mackay, Manasseh had been a brick mason by trade, and following his mission, he did brickwork on the Salt Lake Temple. He also built the giant smokestack in Murray—a landmark of the community for generations.

"Penny for your thoughts," a voice from across the room whispered, breaking the solitude into which Byron had wandered.

"Oh . . . good morning, Avril. I was just thinking of my marvelous ancestors and how much easier I have it than did they."

"Don't know much about my kin folks," Avril sighed, slowly positioning himself so that he could look directly over to where Byron lay. "Fact is, I don't think they ever even kept a record of things."

"That's too bad, Avril. The reason I feel so close to mine is that they kept journals. They left a piece of themselves behind, and I am a better man for it. My wife and I have decided that we'll write down the things that happen in our lives, and perhaps one day a word or two will help somebody else out."

"Did I hear my name mentioned?"

Turning, Byron was pleasantly surprised to see Caryl walking into the room.

"Morning, dear," he smiled, grasping his wife's hand as she leaned over to greet him with a kiss.

"You two don't mind me," Avril interjected. "Fact is, ma'am, I'd be most grateful if you were to pull these here curtains. I sort of need my privacy, if it's okay."

"Of course," Caryl replied, smiling kindly at her husband's new friend. She was impressed with the innocent, childlike manner of Byron's roommate, and was happy that Byron had someone to visit with.

Efficiently, she then drew the curtain past the man's bed and settled into the chair next to Byron. Without a pause, she gave him an update of their children's activities and shared her experience of the previous night. She had prayed for hours, asking that, if it be Heavenly Father's will, Byron be relieved of his pain—even if this meant dying.

As she spoke, Caryl noticed that Byron was able to rub his toes against the sheets, something he had been unable to do for the past several months. She also noticed his empty food tray and knew that, from the breakfast he had just finished eating, his appetite had returned. In short, she was overwhelmed with the immediate healing that was taking place within her husband's body.

As Byron heard Caryl's words and felt of the urgency in her voice, he was deeply moved. He could hardly believe that the Lord had given him such an exceptional companion.

"Thank you, Caryl, for giving so much of yourself. Sometimes I can hardly believe you're real. You know," he continued, feeling an urgency to share his own experience, "I've also had a most remarkable night, and I just have to tell you about it."

"Oh, please do, Byron! Please tell me what's happening!"

And so, in the hour that followed, Byron recounted the events of the previous night and of the miraculous change that had taken place in his heart. Both he and Caryl wept, several times feeling a bonding that was difficult for either to describe. Yes, theirs was a beautiful relationship and with the Lord's help, there was nothing they couldn't do together. They would survive this ordeal. Although they both sensed that Byron's career at Winder Dairy was at a close, they would prayerfully consider their future and the new world of opportunity awaiting them.

After Caryl had left for work, Byron turned over to make himself comfortable. He gazed out the window at the snow-covered trees before him. Immediately, he found himself re-living a day in his early teen years that had completely and eternally changed his life. It was the day he first noticed Caryl Nielson.

The year was 1942, and he was beginning his first day of junior high. Of course, it was in the same Monroe School he had attended since first grade. But things had changed. The new seventh graders from Whittier Elementary had joined them, and Caryl was one of these new students. Byron had felt something special toward this remarkably attractive blond girl the first time he gazed into the beautiful blue eyes, and they soon became fast friends.

As these memories whirled around in his mind, Byron remembered being elected head boy that year and that Shirley Greenwood had been elected head girl. Caryl had often told him that she had wished that she had been the one elected so they could have worked together.

"Cute," he whispered audibly. "Cute" was how she had described him to her friends. And the word had gotten back to him, too, which only deepened his feelings for her.

He remembered Mrs. Frahm's history and geography class, and how he would turn sideways in his chair, just to look at Caryl. As he caught her eye, they would smile at each other. That was how he had known that she liked him and, of course, how Caryl knew that he liked her!

Their affection for one another grew, and toward the end of their eighth-grade year their formal romance began. At their school, it had been tradition for one of the teachers to borrow an old truck, which would be used to transport the eighth graders out to the municipal swimming pool on Fifth North and Second West. The plan was to swim for a couple of hours and then to attend a movie before returning home.

And so the kids piled into the back of the truck, with

Caryl conveniently sitting right next to Byron. They laughed and giggled with their classmates, and before they knew it, they were at the pool, having the time of their lives. Byron especially enjoyed dunking Caryl, letting her know how strong he was.

After playing these games for a time, Byron faced Caryl, and mustering all the boldness he could, he said, "Caryl, if you'll dive off the diving board in the deep end of the pool, I'll buy your ticket into the movie." That had been his way of telling her that she was his sweetheart, since he didn't have the nerve to say it outright.

Nor did Caryl disappoint him. Before she could change her mind, she jumped out of the pool, climbed the diving board ladder, and dove head-first into the deep end.

Byron chuckled to himself as he recalled her coming up out of the water, all smiles.

"Is that a grimace or a smile?"

Startled back to the present, Byron looked up to see Caryl standing over him. "Wha . . . what are you doing back here?"

"I forgot my purse. Besides, I just had to see you again, sweetheart, and tell you how very much I love you. I'm just so humbled at the way your priesthood blessing has changed things."

"Well, now aren't you just the most beautiful girl in the whole world!"

"You're just prejudiced, Byron, and you know it. Now, tell me what you were grinning about when I walked in."

"Actually, dear, I was thinking of how you looked seven long years ago when you came up out of the water, after taking my dare."

"You mean at our eighth-grade swimming party?"

"Yeah, the day I knew you loved me."

"Well, the day we knew we liked each other, anyway, you old romantic."

"Do you recall what happened at the movie, Caryl?"

"You mean when you had to spend ten cents on two tickets, instead of just a nickel? Or are you referring to the moment you nervously put your arm around me?"

"Well, you didn't do anything to remove it," he teased, remembering the newness of emotion that he had felt during that movie.

"Do you remember the name of the movie, Byron?"

"Well, to tell you the truth, I don't. I was kind of preoccupied, if you know what I mean."

"It was the comedy, *Beautiful But Broke*, with Joan Davis. The only thing I remember is that we laughed and laughed, it was so funny."

"Yeah, it was that," Byron sighed, reliving the magic of that first hour with Caryl.

"From that night on," Caryl smiled, "we both knew we were going together, didn't we? You were just so cute that I couldn't get you out of my mind."

"I'll have to admit that I was pretty well smitten, hon. I told the boys that you were my girl and that they'd better not get any fancy ideas about you."

"Remember the ninth-grade elections? You were running for student body president, and I was running for vice president."

"Boy, do I remember that!" Byron answered emphatically. "We both won in the primaries, and then two days before the final election one of the Rushton girls sent me a love letter, saying, `I love you. Do you love me?' I remember writing back, saying, `No, because I love Caryl.'"

"Yes, I remember. I was flattered when I heard about your letter, but that swung the entire election. She had some friends vote against you, and you lost."

"Yeah, by eleven votes. Well, that wouldn't have mattered, either, but you won vice president, and so I had to watch you working all year without me there with you.

We had fun together, though. School dances, class parties, topping beets, eating lunch together. That was a great year."

"I remember," Caryl interrupted, "that on our last day in the beet fields, as you were climbing into the truck, you turned around and smiled at me. I'm not sure that I ever told you this, but in my mind, as clear as could be, a voice told me, "Byron will be a bishop some day.""

"Now that you mention it, I remember you telling me that. In fact, if my memory serves me correctly, you told me that the night we became engaged. I still think you had been in the sun too long to think straight!"

Both laughed and gazed lovingly into each other's eyes.

"Say," Byron continued, changing the subject, "do you remember Mr. Smith?"

"The principal?" Caryl beamed. "How could I forget Mr. Smith?"

"Remember the time we went into his office together, and he said, 'Byron, why don't you just marry the girl?'"

"Yes," Caryl laughed. "We had gone to his office to get some thumb tacks and tape to help us decorate for the Freshman Frolic."

"Well, anyway," Byron continued, "that's the minute I decided I would marry you."

"You've never told me that, honey. All I remember thinking is that I loved you, but that it was puppy love since I was too young to really love you."

For a moment, the two of them just smiled at each other, their hands firmly clasped. Finally, breaking the silence, Caryl continued. "The hardest part for me, though, was having to go to Cyprus High the next year while you went over to Granite."

"Yes, but as cheerleader, and you had the time of your life!"

"Thanks to that beautiful little car outside. You came over and took me to a lot of the games and dances, remember?"

"How could I forget? Or how could I forget all those dates you had with the football players? Speaking of that '34 Ford outside, how is it running, Caryl?"

"Well, it sputters quite a bit, as you know. But it still gets me here to see you."

"Do you think it'll get us over to City Lunch for chili when I get out of here?"

"That's still our favorite date, isn't it, Byron? That, and going over to John's, for a hamburger and iced mug root beer."

"I figure our business alone has kept both places open— for the past five years, anyway."

Again leaning over and kissing her new-spirited, though still-very-ill husband, Caryl smiled and bid him farewell. She was late for work, and even though she could have reminisced for hours about their unique courtship, she just didn't have that luxury at the moment.

When at last she had gone, Avril spoke from behind his curtain. "That lady of yours is something pretty special, Byron."

"She is that," Byron agreed, still basking in the memories of his youth.

"If I ever find that you've been unkind to her, I'll have to track down that '34 Ford of yours and slash your tires."

"The same goes for your wife, Avril. Mary's a gem. So's your son, Johnny."

Both men laughed, and at that moment two assistants entered the room. Pulling back Avril's curtain, they proceeded to lift him from the bed onto another roller bed. Byron knew how frightened Avril was, since in a just a few moments he would be placed in a body cast that would permanently solidify his muscles and joints into the sitting position. From this day on, Avril would spend his waking hours in a wheelchair.

"Say . . . say a prayer for me, Byron," Avril stammered, as he was rolled from the room. "This is the toughest thing I've ever had to do."

Byron spent the next two hours filled with a myriad of emotions. One minute he was thinking and praying for his new friend, Avril. The next he was questioning his own decision to decline the cast, to rely totally on his wife's impressions and on the priesthood blessing he had received the night before. Although neither his nor Caryl's father had been very active in the Church, still they had supported them through the years, and were proud that they had married in the temple.

At last, heavily sedated and sleeping, Avril was wheeled back into the room, enveloped in a rigid white body cast. Byron ached inside as if he, himself, had been suddenly imprisoned in plaster. But it wasn't him, and he felt that within days he would be walking out of the hospital and driving his Ford home to Granger.

As Byron considered how it would feel to sit again in his car, he returned to a time miles and years away. It was a late June night, between his junior and senior year, and he and Caryl were just returning from a movie. Sitting in front of her home, he kissed her goodnight and then asked, "Caryl, do you think we'll ever get married?"

"Oh, maybe some day," she replied shyly.

"Well, I want to get you a ring."

"Oh, Byron, that would be wonderful. But you'll have to receive permission from my father, you know."

The following night, Byron mustered all the courage he could and headed out to the Nielson's chicken coops, where Caryl's father was doing the chores. Mr. Nielson sensed what was coming, as he had been expecting such a request. And so, determining to do some mischief of his own, he decided to let Byron sweat a bit by not allowing him to ask the question.

Byron followed him around the coops while he did the chores, and Mr. Nielson kept the conversation on everything but Caryl. At last, sensing that Byron's nerves were nearly shot, Mr. Nielson stopped, turned to face the lad, and asked, "Is there something you would like to ask me, Byron?"

"Uh . . . yessir, there is," Byron coughed, feeling more nervous than he had at any time in his entire life. "I . . . uh, was wondering . . . uh . . . if you would mind if . . . uh . . . I was to marry Caryl."

"Well," Mr. Nielson smiled, "you're both a bit young, don't you think?"

"Yessir, we are. But I don't mean right away. We've still got our senior year ahead of us. We could get engaged now, then wait until maybe Christmas to get married."

"Oh, you could get married at Christmas time alright," Mr. Nielson replied casually, carefully selecting his words so as not to offend the boy. "But if you do that, I won't have the money to pay for a wedding reception. On the other hand, if you wait until you've graduated, we could do things up right."

"Uh . . ." Byron stammered, searching for the right words, "that would be fine with us, sir. We're not in any hurry. We just want to get matters all planned out so we can handle things financially."

"You're a fine young man, Byron. Caryl's mother and I have trusted our daughter with you, as you know. And that hasn't been easy, with you being a Granite High Farmer and all."

Both men laughed, easing the tension of the conversation. Then Mr. Nielson, thinking that perhaps he needed to give Byron some reassurance, put his arm around him, and the two walked into the house.

The following weeks were spent looking for just the right diamond, and Byron and Caryl enjoyed the excitement as they spoke with different jewelers. Finally, after selecting just the right one, Byron could hardly wait to officially become engaged.

And so, on the night of August 18, 1947, while seated in his '34 Ford, Byron gave Caryl the ring. Caryl graciously accepted, they kissed, and then before Byron knew it, she disappeared into her home, eager to tell her family that she was going to become Mrs. Byron Mackay.

Their senior year came and went. During that time, Byron's parents gave him a lot next to theirs on 4100 South, just west of Redwood Road, and Byron and Caryl worked hard to build their new little home on it. They dug their own septic tank, and although they had no indoor gas, they installed an oil heater in the small living room. The home had just three main rooms and a bathroom, but to them, it seemed like a mansion. The home cost a total of $4,000 to build, and they had mutually saved $2,600 of this amount. So they had to borrow $1,400 from Byron's father to finish paying for it. Still, their future was bright, and they knew that when they married they would be prepared to begin life as they dreamed it would be.

Now, as Byron's thoughts returned to the present, he wondered if their dream was over and if they would be forced to sell the home they had worked so hard to build. Even though they had repaid his father for the home loan, Byron still had to feed his growing family. And how could he do this when he couldn't even walk into a job interview? Then again, how could he doubt Caryl's faith and the feeling of peace and well-being that he experienced last night?

And so, with new resolve, Byron breathed deeply and offered a silent prayer. Greater miracles than his had been wrought, and if he just had the faith, he knew he could find the answers. Speaking with Heavenly Father, he made a promise to dedicate his life and energies to the Lord, if only he would be blessed with the strength to do so.

The clock near his bed ticked softly, and outside a sparrow landed gently on the window sill. It sat there for a long time, drawing warmth from the sun, as its rays reflected from the ledge. God, the Creator of all, was aware and would certainly shower His blessings. After all, Byron had been foreordained to a certain work, and it had just begun.

• THREE •
LEARNING TO TRUST

Trust in the Lord with all thine heart; and lean not unto thine own understanding. In all thy ways acknowledge him, and he shall direct thy paths. Proverbs 3:5-6

Two weeks later, after spending a full month in the hospital, Byron prepared to return home. Caryl and the kids picked him up at the hospital, and he spent the ride home eagerly anticipating his first day with them. Neither of the children had been able to visit him at the hospital. Being with them again after their long separation filled Byron with unprecedented joy. His heart was full, and he later told Caryl that those moments of reunion contained more joy than he could comprehend.

Byron's health was very tenuous, as the doctors had informed him that his medicine, a crude form of cortisone, was temporarily effective and could only be administered for a ten-day period. They indicated that he should go home, enjoy a few days with his family, and then, when the pain returned, come back to the hospital for a second round of treatments.

And so, knowing that his future was uncertain and that

further hospital confinement would be necessary, Byron returned to Granger, determined to enjoy his days as best he could. Thus, lying on the sofa, he waited for Caryl to bring the kids home, praying with all his heart that he could prove worthy of his blessings.

In a strange way, Byron felt as new to his surroundings as he had when he and Caryl married. The wedding date had been June 4th, the Friday following Caryl's high school graduation. They had enjoyed a beautiful ceremony performed by Brother Robert Burton in the Salt Lake Temple. After the reception, they went to a small restaurant for fried chicken. They then checked into the Capitol Motel, on State Street, for the night. The next morning they drove up Big Cottonwood Canyon to their Uncle Manasseh's cabin at Silver Fork. Manasseh had been named after Byron's great grandfather, Manasseh, and for a wedding present had given them a week at his cabin.

As these memories flooded his mind, Byron closed his eyes, imagining he and Caryl's conversation on their way to the cabin. They had stopped for groceries and were just entering the mouth of the canyon.

Moving slowly up the road so as to not overheat the radiator of their Ford, Byron suddenly spoke, breaking the silence. "Honey," he began, somewhat tentatively, "why do you suppose we weren't even tempted to betray our moral values before marriage?"

"Oh, sweetheart," Caryl sighed, smiling, "I remember when we met that you told me you were the president of your deacon's quorum. Then, by the time we had our first date in the ninth grade, you were president of your teacher's quorum. I knew how important your priesthood was to you, and I had you on such a pedestal that I wouldn't have compromised you for anything in the world."

"That's funny, because I had you on the same pedestal. Your virtue was the most sacred thing in the world to me. I remember thinking that when we had our first kiss. That was a moment that I'll remember as long as I live."

"You know, Byron, that you're the only boy I ever kissed. I just always wanted a kiss to be a sacred event, and not just a social one.

"There was something else, too, Byron," Caryl continued. "As you know, my mother died when I was just six years old. There have been many times that I have felt her spirit and protecting influence. I think that our strength to be true to ourselves and each other came largely through her influence."

"You've never shared those feelings, Caryl. But you know, I think you might be right. The thing we will always know and remember is that we walked into the Lord's House in total worthiness, having never compromised our convictions. I have a feeling that, in the years to come, our beginning will serve as a solid foundation that can't be shattered."

"Oh, Byron, you are so wise. I love you more than ever, darling, and I will always be here to help you realize your dreams."

"I love you, too, sweetheart. Now, if you could open your window, perhaps we can enjoy this pure mountain air."

The week went by, and while Byron and Caryl honeymooned, Byron's sister finished wallpapering and painting their new little home, preparing it for their return.

Byron and Caryl drove back to Granger, wishing that their time together in the mountains would never end, yet realizing that they had to get back to work and to their new little home. On their way home, they took the silver dollars Caryl's father had given them as a wedding gift and purchased venetian blinds for the bay window of their new home.

As Byron recalled those happy, carefree days, he

marveled that so many changes had taken place in the four years that had followed. Trials had been born, many of them, and life was difficult. But two beautiful children had also been born, and his love for Caryl and his growing family continued to deepen.

After ten days of convalescing and a very faith-promoting family fast, Byron's mother and his sister, Elva, drove him back to the county hospital. Even though it was very difficult to accept, he was fully prepared to be re-admitted and to resume cortisone treatments.

Dr. Samuelson met Byron at the door, but instead of admitting him, the doctor excitedly informed Byron that an even newer medicine, called Buta-Zolodin, had been discovered, and was available in pill form. The doctor informed Byron that he was only the nineteenth patient to try it. He indicated that this medicine was not for use on the open medical market, but could only be administered on a strictly controlled, trial basis.

Needless to say, Byron and the others were elated. And so, after taking the first dosage of these pills, and with a supply tucked safely inside a sack beside him, Byron returned home to Granger. Because Caryl had no knowledge of his early return, he decided to surprise her. He would be in the house, and when she returned home from work, he would be standing in the doorway to greet her. To this point, he had been completely confined to a wheelchair for five weeks. He had felt an immediate response to the medicine, though, and was determined to greet Caryl by walking toward her the moment she opened the door.

After several hours of solitude, Byron could at last hear the familiar whine of the Ford's engine as Caryl drove up the dirt road that led to the front door. At that moment, he couldn't remember ever hearing a sweeter sound. He had only paid $175 cash for the Ford back when he was a sopho-more in high school, but on this day six years later, it sounded more like a thousand dollar Bentley!

Struggling to his feet, Byron slowly took one step, then two, making his way toward the back door. When Caryl saw him walking toward her, she flew into his arms, thrilled beyond words, yet demanding to know why he was home and how could he possibly be walking. When at last Byron had finished explaining and had shown Caryl the new pills, both sat back on the sofa and marveled at how truly blessed they were. A miracle had taken place, and both were eager to acknowledge the Lord's intervention in Byron's behalf.

A month passed. Byron took this new medicine and gathered pounds and strength. One day, as he was convalescing, he received word from the County Rehabilitation Center. They were concerned for Byron's future employment possibilities, knowing that he could neither remain standing nor sitting for any length of the time. He would have to choose a profession where he could move about from one position to another.

Responding with optimism, Byron went into their office to consider his possible employment opportunities. He began to interview with prospective employers, sensing a need to at least begin working somewhere. But, for one reason or another, no jobs were offered to him, and he and Caryl became more discouraged than ever. He was just grateful that they had paid back the $1,400 loan on their home. They were living on the $80 a month that Caryl made doing books at the dairy, but that wasn't enough. More and more they found themselves the recipients of farm produce and groceries from their family and friends. It was very difficult for them to learn to receive. But they felt their situation presented an opportunity to grow, and so they didn't murmur. Instead, they continued to pray, hoping that Byron would find a way to take advantage of his improved health.

One day, while lying on the sofa, Byron began browsing through a magazine, as much to divert his mind from the pain he was in as anything else. After several minutes of reading, he saw something that caught his attention.

"Look at this, Caryl!" he said excitedly, holding out the magazine for his wife to examine.

"Look at what?" Caryl asked, not understanding.

"That picture. See that picture? It's a barber, a hair cutter. I think I could become a barber, honey!"

"Well, maybe you could, Byron. Your dad cut your hair and taught you to do it. And Glen isn't any worse off for how you've cut his hair, so I think you should give it a try."

"I've seen those swivel chairs that barbers sometimes use, and between the chair and standing, I think I could make enough to care for our needs."

And so, with hope in their hearts, Caryl drove Byron into Salt Lake, passing the inspiring temple on their way to the Salt Lake Barber College, located on 51 East 200 South.

When they walked into the college and introduced themselves, Byron was very weak. But though his hands were in pain and were totally out of shape, he was determined to realize his newfound goal. He could quietly live with the pain, and trusted that if only he could put his hands to use, the strength would return.

With great reluctance, the school administrators finally admitted Byron to their program. They were very concerned that he would not have the strength and endurance to begin such a career and yet, sensing his determined spirit, allowed him to begin with the other 13 students. The $270 tuition was paid by the state rehabilitation program, and so the only obstacle left for Byron to overcome was the rigors of the training.

At last, after being out of school for several years, Byron began his first day as a student. For five days a week, he would arise and have Caryl assist him with dressing and breakfast. He would then catch a ride into the city and attend school. It was terribly exhausting, and yet somehow he found the strength to persevere.

Finally, after six long and difficult months, Byron completed the course and prepared for the final examination. He had passed the written portion, and now had to prove his skills by cutting various heads of hair, each with a different style.

The test was a great ordeal, and Byron collapsed that night, completely exhausted. The pressure, as well as the physical strain, was almost unbearable. Still, he was confident that he had passed the practical portion of the exam. His mood changed, however, when he was informed several days later that he had not passed the test. Both he and Caryl were devastated. They just couldn't comprehend it, since he had averaged 98 percent on all of the written tests and, in spite of the rigors of the practical test, had felt good about his competency in actual barbering. When at last Byron summoned the courage to call the administrators and inquire as to why he had failed, he was more discouraged than ever. They explained that he had not been able to stand straight enough, and that his hands were so misshapen that they feared he would not be able to cut hair with quality.

This was a blow that was almost more than either Byron or Caryl, could take. Still, with so much invested, and with a feeling of hope in knowing that the Lord had placed this opportunity before him, Byron pressed to have this ruling overturned. He had become competent, and he could succeed as a barber, so surely an exception could be made.

The officials at the rehabilitation center also became involved, and with their insistence, the ruling was finally overturned. Byron, overcoming almost insurmountable odds, received his license to barber. When he and Caryl received word of this decision, they felt overwhelmed with gratitude, knowing that Heavenly Father had heard and answered their prayers.

Byron received his diploma at the graduation ceremonies,

April 13, 1953. Written on the diploma was the fact that he had completed a thousand hours of training. Both Byron and Caryl returned to Granger that day sensing that, in spite of their many trials, they had been blessed and that, with the Lord's help, there was nothing they could not accomplish in their future.

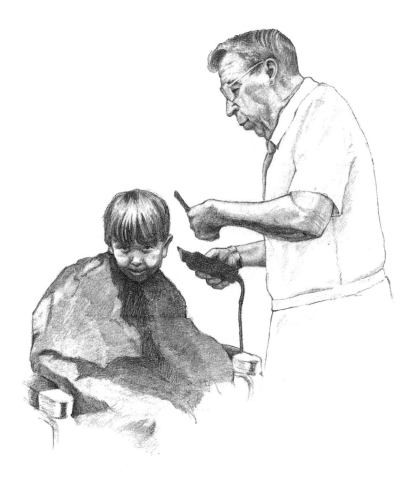

• FOUR •
A REAL "CUT-UP"

Seek ye first the kingdom of God, and his righteousness; and all these things shall be added unto you. Matthew 6:33

Almost immediatcly, Byron was hired as an apprentice at Clary's Barber Shop, on 3500 South and 3800 West, in Salt Lake County. Haircuts cost up to $3.50, and Byron was able to take $1.25 as his split. Of course, because he was second chair and had to take the overflow customers, he began his business by cutting only two or three heads of hair a day. This seemed such a small contribution to his family's finances, but Byron had confidence that his business would grow and eventually provide for the needs of his growing family.

His business did grow, and before long, he found himself cutting 20 to 25 heads of hair a day. He had formed special friendships with many of his customers and felt that he had truly become an important part of their lives. He learned of their activities, their hardships, and their joys and found his ability to love and to care increasing daily.

Not surprisingly, one of Byron's customers was his friend from the hospital, Avril. Avril had successfully worn the cast and had permanently assumed a sitting position. This made it difficult for Avril to get around, and so twice a month Byron would drive over to Avril's home and cut his hair for him. Avril had become an accomplished lawn mower repairman, and so they would sit and visit in his repair shop while Byron cut his hair.

One day as this ritual was being repeated, Byron paused, looked into Avril's eyes, and asked, "Avril, do you regret your decision to spend your life in a wheelchair?"

"Actually, Byron, I don't know if I do, or not. I know that I'm not in a great deal of pain and that I can maneuver around quite well, but still I miss walking and running and doing things with my wife and son. I just wish they'd have let me try that new medicine like they let you."

"Well, you had been in your cast for almost a month by that time, Avril. Maybe the Lord allowed you to go through life this way so that you wouldn't go so fast that you couldn't serve him."

"Maybe he did, Byron, although my bishop hasn't asked me to accept a job in the ward. How about you? Do you have a church job?"

"Actually I do, Avril. I've been M-Men President for some time now, working with the young Aaronic Priesthood boys. It's great, too, although I certainly can't keep up with them. We laugh about it a lot, but they know I do what I can, and that makes it okay with them."

"Maybe I'm just not meant for service, Byron. I just can't see myself doing something like that."

"Well, you're a ward teacher, aren't you? That's the most important church calling, you know."

"Yeah, I suppose so. My bishop gave me the Jones family to teach, and since they live next door, it works out quite well. Still, I just don't see me and my wheelchair being of much use."

"Some time ago, I wrote something down in the front

cover of my journal, Avril, and I think it might apply to both of us. It goes like this: `Success, or making a contribution, sometimes requires that we have faith in ourselves, even when no one else does.'"

"Seems right, Byron, although I don't rightly know if I even understand what faith is."

For the next half hour, Byron shared his insights about the principle of faith as he continued to cut Avril's hair. Before leaving, he challenged Avril to think of each one of his customers as needing sharpening and fine tuning, just as their lawn mowers did. He invited his friend to always send his customers away feeling better about themselves than when they arrived.

Now, driving home in his old but trusted Ford, Byron quietly offered a prayer of thanks—both for knowing such a fine man as Avril, and for being able to speak so openly with him. After all, their conversations always seemed to be more important than the hair cut.

Two years after being paid for his first barbering, Byron received his Master Barber designation. He would have to pay a rental fee for his chair from that time forward, but he would be able to take home the balance of what he charged, enabling him to more easily meet the needs of his family. By this time, their third child, Dan Byron, had been born, and so their expenses had increased proportionately. Still, they always seemed to have enough to go around and to give their kids a good Christmas. They recognized that the Lord was truly blessing them.

One of Byron's favorite customers was Ned Winder, the nephew of his former boss, George Winder. Byron loved to see Ned pull up outside the shop, because he knew that everyone was in for a treat. Ned was always laughing and kidding around, and his visit on this day would prove no exception.

"Good morning, Byron," Ned smiled, as he entered the

shop. "Glad you boys are open today, after the way it rained last night."

"Well," Byron answered, climbing out of the chair so that Ned could sit down for his cut, "we almost got washed away, but things look pretty bright out there this morning."

"Brought us a bit of refreshment," Ned continued, holding up a quart of Winder milk and a sack of sweet rolls. "If you have the cups, we can all have a midmorning treat."

"Have we got cups!" Clary interrupted, leaving his customer, Tom Black, to retrieve four small glasses from the back room. "I figured that being unprepared last time was enough. We'll always have cups."

The men cheerfully consumed the milk and pastries Ned had provided, savoring each swallow of the snack as though it was their last. Ned smiled knowingly that he had long ago made Clary and Byron believers in the exquisite refreshment that only Winder milk and bakery products could provide.

"You own a bakery out there, too?" Tom asked, at last breaking the silence.

"Yes, and a cemetery, too. Our motto is `Drink our milk and eat our bread. Then let us bury you when you're dead.'"

The four men laughed, Ned's haircut began, and each enjoyed the merriment that this unusual friend brought into the shop.

"Say, Ned," Byron asked, venturing into a new conversation, "I've always wanted to ask you how you keep your shoes so shiny?"

"And your car," Clary interrupted, smiling. "Every one else in Granger generally has a dusty car, especially when it rains. But not you. Your car and your shoes are always as shiny as a brand new penny!"

"Well, boys, it's not that hard, actually. You see my crooked finger here? My dad says it was made that way so I could put a good spit-shine on my shoes. He's always told me that you can tell a whole lot about someone by the way he cleans his shoes and his car. As for my car, washing it off each morning is just a bit of therapy for me. Sort of gets my mind in gear for what I have to do that day. My wife, Gwennie, has come to expect it, and I don't dare disappoint her. I figure if I at least keep myself and the car looking good, she'll have a hard time leaving me."

Again the men laughed, and by the time Ned and Tom had left the shop, Byron and Clary knew they were going to have a good day.

And it was a good day, too. For Byron, though, the capstone came after work, when he was invited to meet with a member of the stake presidency. He had been asked to serve as secretary in the elder's quorum presidency, and he felt humbled with the call. It was becoming increasingly hard for him to hold a pencil and to write, but he knew that with the Lord's help he could keep the records and reports as the Lord would expect him to. For Byron, there was just no other way.

PART TWO

THE REFINER'S FRIENDS

After having successfully "passed through" the Refiner's Fire, it becomes opportune for the sons and daughters of man to be made clean, pure, and spotless—in essence, to be sanctified. As this process of sanctification takes place, the Savior is then able to declare, through the Holy Spirit, His new friendship with those persons.

From the perception of those around them, Byron and Caryl's evolving integrity allowed them the blessing of this unique, vibrant, and everlasting friendship.

• FIVE •
A DECADE OF STRETCHING

And prove me now herewith, saith the Lord of hosts, if I will not open you the windows of heaven, and pour you out a blessing, that there shall not be room enough to receive it. Malachi 3:10

December 31, 1979

As the sun quietly set to the west, Byron turned the key to his barber shop and walked slowly to his car. He loved the beauty of the sunset, and this evening was no different. The last rays fell gracefully on the snow-covered field before him, and he was again reminded of the truly miraculous blessings that were his, not the least of which was his very own business—Byron's Barber Shop. He had been barbering for twenty-five years, a full quarter of a century, and yet somehow it had seemed like only a few months ago that he had cut his first head of hair.

As he climbed into the '72 Plymouth they had purchased the previous June, he sat and reflected on the small, seventeen-year-old brown building before him. He had enjoyed his years working at Clary's shop until that time, and had built up a very dedicated clientele. He was averaging twenty-five to thirty cuts a day, and felt that his customers would follow him to his new location. Then, in 1963, he had the opportunity to open his own barber shop and to enjoy creating his own business climate. It was simply too enticing for him to pass up.

He and Caryl had an opportunity to purchase a small parcel of land, located near 3200 West and 3500 South. It was closer to home and offered a central location for his business. Obstacles presented themselves, however, as the county was very resolute about not granting him a building permit. This didn't deter, Byron, however. He knew George Anast, who owned a grocery store, and who was a very prominent businessman in the area.

One day, while speaking with George, he expressed his desire to have his own shop, and to his surprise, George answered, "Well, Byron, if you want to open your own barber shop, I'll build you one. I'm going to build a group of retail stores, anyway, just west of Redwood Road on 3500 South, and we'll just make one of them a barber shop."

So, with George applying for the building permit, it sailed right through the building committee. Within a few short weeks, he had built the freestanding building that would become Byron's second home. George had given him his choice of either buying the building or renting it, and indicated that the payment would be $85 a month, either way. The total purchase price was $15,000, with a very low interest rate. He and Caryl took about sixty seconds to decide which way to go. They each experienced a sense of accomplishment, knowing that they could own their business and building. Byron appreciated George's helping hand, and was greatly humbled by this act of kindness.

Returning to the present, Byron started the car and pulled out into the street. As he traveled along Redwood Road toward his home, his thoughts reflected on the blessing his four beautiful children were. His youngest daughter, Sandra, had been born three years after Dan's birth, in 1957. That was twenty-two years ago, and she had truly become the crowning jewel of his fatherhood. Heavenly Father should send everyone a daughter as the youngest child, he reasoned. His goal, he now understood, was to be as worthy as his children were and to lead them in righteousness. Byron felt overwhelmed as he considered the magnitude of that responsibility but drove home knowing the Lord would give him the strength to fulfill it.

Later that evening, after finishing dinner, Caryl spoke. "Byron, why don't you go into the family room and lie down while I do the dishes. I'll join you in just a few minutes."

"Honey," Byron smiled, "I wish that I could. But my assistants are waiting for me over at the church, and we've got to reorganize our home teaching assignments."

"But, sweetheart, you've got to take better care of yourself. Can't you miss just this one meeting?"

"Oh, I could, alright," Byron agreed, pulling himself slowly to his feet. "But the Lord didn't call me to be High Priest Group Leader just to let the others do the work. Besides, I'm feeling somewhat better this evening, and I need to take advantage of that."

"Well, then I'll help you get dressed," Caryl sighed, knowing there was no way to keep her husband home when the Lord's work needed to be done. "I just ironed your new white shirt, and it's waiting for you to try it on."

As Caryl assisted Byron into his new Christmas shirt and tie, her heart was suddenly touched by the continued courage of her husband in spite of the decade of illnesses and surgeries he had endured.

"Do you realize," she suddenly asked, breaking the silence, "that it has been almost ten years since your first hip operation?"

"I was thinking of that the other day, actually. Those

thirty-one days in the old St. Mark's Hospital were no picnic, were they?"

"Well," Caryl added, "they wouldn't have been too bad if you had not had to spend twenty-one of them in traction."

"Kept me out of mischief, though, didn't it, Little Susy?"

They both laughed as Byron used his favorite nickname for his wife, and then Caryl remembered something else. "Peggy's boyfriend, Michael, was serving his mission in Denmark, and Glen was back in school at the University of Utah. At least lying there in the hospital gave you time to catch up on your letter writing."

"I'm afraid my crippled fingers kept me from writing very many letters, Caryl. But I sure thought of those boys a lot. Glen had been so happy out there, and in a strange way, I always felt like he was representing me, since I hadn't gone on a mission."

"I think the Lord knew we needed to start our family early, Byron, and that was why you weren't called. I've always felt that way."

"You may be right, Caryl. Sometimes it seems like my mission is to endure pain and never-ending surgeries."

"It's interesting, hon, that every three years you've gone back into the hospital. First it was your hip replacement and then, in '73, your knee was operated on."

"Yes," Byron laughed, "and in the off years, the kids went on missions. Dan left for Brazil in '74, while Sandra was a junior over at Cottonwood High. Then, after she graduated, I went to the new St. Mark's for my second knee operation."

"That was after Elio had left, wasn't it, Byron?"

"Yes, he stayed with us from January until June, and the surgery was in the fall."

"I wonder how Elio is doing," Caryl sighed, remembering the exchange student from Brazil they had taken into their home. Dan was just finishing his mission to Brazil during the time Elio had lived with them, and he was so proud that they had taken a Brazilian into their home.

"Oh, he'll do well wherever he goes," Byron concluded, smiling. "Now, walk me to the car, Little Susy, and I'll be getting on over to the church."

A few minutes later, as she straightened the kitchen, Caryl found herself remembering Elio Micheloni, who had been such a thoughtful young man. She recalled how she had been directed by the Holy Spirit to inquire about the exchange program and to offer to open their home to a foreign exchange student. She and Byron knew that having an additional person in their home would not prevent her from continuing her service as Stake Relief Society President. The five months he was there were spent in learning and in teaching. She would always be thankful for Elio, and she offered a silent prayer for his continued well-being.

Later that night, after Caryl had fallen asleep, Byron found himself staring into the dark void above his bed. He just couldn't relax his mind enough to sleep. His thoughts jumped from the present back to when Elio had lived with them. Elio's stay was followed by the acceptance of a second Brazilian exchange student, Rosana Falcao. She had lived with them at the time of Byron's second hip replacement, and then the third, when his first artificial hip had worn out and needed to be replaced. Those hospital stays were difficult. But even more challenging were the agonizing days afterward, when he would have to learn to walk all over again, and struggle through the physical pain of returning to work to manage his barber shop.

As Byron thought of his shop, his mind floated back to a day during that same time period, when he was again cutting Ned Winder's hair. The county had informed him that they were widening the street in front of his shop and that he would need to move his building at least twenty feet to the rear, onto additional property they had to buy from George. But, of course, Byron had no way to pay for this move. The county had reimbursed him $19,000 for part of the move, but the expenses would be $23,000, and he had nowhere to turn. He just didn't have the means to borrow the $4,000 difference.

Then one of his customers, Clarence "Cad" Shafer, a contractor who was also a member of the Granger Stake High Council, came to him. Cad had learned of Byron's plight and told Byron that the Lord had told him to move the building back and to not charge Byron for it. And to think that Cad's wife, Ruth, was in bed recovering from knee operations with casts on both legs. All this, and Cad still took time to help Byron. Cad even went to the extent of enlisting the help of his colleagues, Bud Rich, a counselor in the stake presidency, to install all of the plumbing, and Bob Beecher, an architect who drew up the plans. They then got everything passed through the city planning and zoning departments. Still another, Kay Christiansen, helped Cad move the building. Cad and the others had really given their all so that Byron could continue to provide for his family.

Byron had been able to pay for some of the work the other men did, and he was thankful that they had accepted the money, even though it was only a small fraction of the amount he knew they could rightfully charge. But Cad would accept nothing—either for himself or for his son, Ernie.

Remembering how difficult it was to accept this selfless gift from Cad, Byron spoke with Ned Winder about it that afternoon as he was finishing Ned's haircut. At that time, the building had been moved back onto its new foundation, and Cad's son, Ernie, was outside installing a handrail that would assist Byron into his shop.

"You mean," Ned had inquired, "that Cad poured your

new foundation, then moved your shop back onto it, without charging you a cent?"

"That's what I'm saying, Ned. He and his boy have spent three weeks working full-time to get this job done. Cad says the Lord will pay him for doing it. The problem for me is that I just can't let him do it. It's not right to take advantage of someone like that, even when they offer. I've made out a check for $150, and I'm going to give it to Ernie when he comes in."

"Seems to me," Ned continued, not hearing Byron's words, "that the Lord's looking down on two of his sons, and has decided to help both of you."

"Uh . . . I'm not sure I follow you, Ned."

"Well, I think Cad has it right when he says that he'll be richly blessed by doing this for you. But I also think the reverse is true. My grandfather, John R. Winder, when he was a counselor in the First Presidency to Joseph F. Smith, made the statement that learning to receive at the hands of others is every bit as valuable as learning to give. Now, how can you deny Cad, or yourself, the opportunity of receiving these blessings?"

At that moment, Ernie opened the front door, knocked the dirt off of his shoes, and entered. "I think the sidewalk is dry enough to walk on, Byron, and if I could just get a drink of water, I'll tear off the concrete forms."

Pulling out the check for $150, Byron extended his crippled hand and said, "Here, Ernie. I want you to have this."

But Ernie refused to take the check, waving it off with his hand.

"Ernie," Byron pressed, "I insist that you take this money!"

Ernie glanced over to Ned, winked, and said, "Byron, I'm going home if you're going to talk like that."

With that, Ernie poured a cup of water, turned, and exited the shop. Byron started to follow him, but Ned jumped to his feet, grabbed him by the shoulders, and turned him around. Then, looking him directly in the eye, with tears forming in his own eyes, Ned repeated, "Byron, don't deny him the blessing of giving!"

Feeling exasperated, yet knowing there was nothing he could do, Byron replied, "I suppose you're right, Ned, although sometimes I wish the good Lord would pass me by for a while and let someone else enjoy a few of these blessings."

The two men laughed, breaking the tension in the air. Then, after giving his usual generous tip, Ned put on his hat, walked out the door, and climbed into his shiny maroon car. Waving goodbye, he drove east, heading for work at the Church Office Building. He had been Executive Secretary of the Missionary Department since his return from presiding over the Florida Mission in '66, and he always spoke of his missionary days as the choicest of his life.

As the car disappeared from view, Byron coughed, clearing his throat. He loved Ned, and marveled once again at how his perspective had been changed with just a few well-placed words. If only he could have the same impact as he shared his thoughts and impressions with those who found their way to his shop. It was certainly a goal to reach for, and if the good Lord would just allow all of his artificial joints to work, he would continue to serve, in whatever way he could.

The following morning, while waiting for the New Year's Day football games to begin, Byron listened with interest to the sound of his son-in-law, Michael, shoveling the snow from his driveway. Michael and Peggy lived not far away and were hoping to build a home behind theirs so that they could better care for Byron and Caryl's needs.

"Mike is such a great son-in-law," Byron whispered audibly to himself. "He works so hard on his route with Winder Dairy, then comes by every day to check on me and help me out. I know the good Lord sent Michael to our family every bit as much for me, as for Peggy—especially since Glen was the one who encouraged Mike to write to Peggy while he was serving his mission in Virginia."

That thought made Byron grin, and with Macy's New Year Parade unfolding on T.V., he worked his way back in his recliner. He could hear Caryl in the kitchen, preparing a large dinner for the family. How could he have ever been fortunate enough to have found a companion like Caryl? Thank goodness she was feeling better and that her heart was functioning well.

"How would you like some orange juice?"

Opening his eyes, Byron looked up to see Caryl standing over him, a large glass of juice in her hand.

"Thanks, Little Susy. I was just thinking of your great heart and how thankful I am that it's not giving you problems."

"I can't believe that it's been almost two years since my open-heart surgery, Byron. We were forty-seven years old at the time, and I would think that now I'm good for at least another forty-seven years!"

"You'd think that my problems were enough, Caryl, and that the Lord would show us a little mercy."

"He has, Byron. Sometimes it feels like a very little mercy, but mostly I feel like the most blessed woman I know."

"I'd really like to browse through the pages of your journal, Caryl. Would you mind handing it to me?"

"How could I mind? I'm flattered to think that you enjoy reading it. Was there any particular part that you wanted to refer to?"

"Actually there was. I just wanted to go back and read what you had to say about your operation and about our trials. You have a way of putting things that gives me quite a bit of hope, you know."

Stooping down and kissing her husband, Caryl handed him the juice and then retrieved her journal from the bedroom. Opening it, she turned to the creased page and then leafed back two pages.

"Here, honey, read this. I was waxing a bit philosophical when I wrote this. It'll give you an idea of what I was thinking before I learned of my heart problems."

Thanking her and handing back the empty juice glass, Byron carefully took the large white journal and worked his gnarled fingers around the open pages. Thank goodness Caryl is blind to my deformities, he considered, or she'd see that my fingers are really looking bad. But then, that was Caryl, always looking for the good in him and never seeing the down side. He was grateful that she had never spoken of his increasing deformities; instead, she just held his hands whenever she could, making him feel as though he was the most handsome man in all of Granger.

Page 11 of Caryl's journal, written May 17, 1977, read as follows:

Earlier I explained of Byron's condition, and I continue here to tell of a great trial—but because of faith, prayers and humility, and a realization that we must be submissive to our Heavenly Father's will, we are able to receive His blessings and desires for us.

Byron has been under great stress and pain since January. Both hips were giving him trouble, but the left one became very painful. He was finally scheduled for surgery on April 20th. However, four days before this Dr. Lamb's nurse called and said that the doctor had to leave Salt Lake to testify at a court trial in the east. So, Byron's surgery was rescheduled for May 4th.

This was a great concern to us because we could see that Byron was failing, losing weight from pain, etc. But somehow we made it through the next two weeks. The last week he slept in his clothes on the sofa in the family room, with just an afghan over him. He was in such pain that he slept only occasionally, and going to work was also very wearing on him.

The Thursday before he was to enter the hospital, a rash appeared on his left leg—the one to be operated on. We called Dr. Lamb's nurse, Marie, and after she consulted with a doctor, she told us that this would not prevent surgery.

Byron grew worse daily. When he entered St. Mark's Hospital on May 2nd, he was in terrible pain, and was physically exhausted.

The night before surgery, I had to attend a Relief Society leadership meeting. It had been an extremely trying week, with Byron's condition worsening daily, and with my having to prepare for this meeting. I felt strongly that we deserved a special blessing. We were serving the Lord, doing our best to live the gospel, raising a family— Glen and Dan had both served missions. Maybe it was necessary to prove my faith to my Heavenly Father.

Byron's rash grew worse, and a Doctor Elledge determined that it was "shingles." He indicated that he would decide that night whether to proceed with the surgery.

I prayed fervently, and fasted that day. That night, during the Relief Society meeting that I conducted, I bore my testimony, and asked the 100+ sisters in attendance to pray also, that Byron would be able to overcome the problems he was having, and be able to have the surgery the next day. I had absolute faith that with my faith, and that of the sisters, the way would be cleared for Byron's surgery, and his release from his painful condition.

After the meeting, I went to the hospital, and learned that the doctors were consulting about whether or not to proceed. After some time, Doctor Lamb came into the room and said, "No surgery. Byron will be going home for two weeks."

Needless to say, I was crushed. I went home and cried in anguish of heart and soul. To think that Byron would be sent home in such a condition. We had both gone to our physical and mental limits to get to the point where he would be able to endure surgery. But now that was cancelled, and I felt abandoned. Not that I doubted Heavenly Father's being there, but for some reason we were left to struggle alone. Why?! Why?!

As Byron completed his second page of reading, he found himself struggling to hold back the tears. Removing his glasses, he took a deep breath and wondered how they had survived that time in their lives. He closed his eyes for a moment, reliving the ordeal again and again in his mind. Then, working his glasses back onto his face, he continued.

Byron came home the next day, fortified with a strong prescription of prednisone. Within three days he began feeling better. His pain eased, and he began to eat and to rest. The shingles, which had caused him even more pain, started to disappear, and gradually a real transformation began. Byron was growing stronger daily, and it was a wonderful, unexpected change. Slowly, I began to see that what had happened was not coincidental, but a direct blessing from the Lord.

Doctor Elledge told me later that because of Byron's weakened condition, he likely would not have survived the surgery—especially if the shingles had attacked the new hip area. I came to realize this to be true. If Heavenly Father had allowed my faith to get in the way of His wisdom, the consequences would have been very different.

Is it any wonder that we "know" the Savior and Heavenly Father are real, and that they do love us? Jesus suffered so much more than any of us have suffered. He feels for our pain, and loves us when we experience our adversities. Earth life is a school of adversity and happiness and learning. We may not understand now, but someday we will. I know this—it's a promise!

For a second time, Byron placed the journal in his lap and closed his eyes. Little had Caryl known as she had penned these words how much she would have to heed her own counsel in the months following.

As Byron lay back in his recliner, he recalled the first time Caryl had been admitted to St. Mark's Hospital for pneumonia. It was June 18th, just two years earlier. The previous February she had felt great fatigue from her Church callings, having served for fifteen years in heavy leadership assignments. She had served the first five of these as Ward Relief Society President and Primary Inservice Leader, and the last ten as Stake Relief Society President. At that time, because of her own poor health as well as the great burden of caring for Byron, she felt she should be released.

But President Peter "Pete" Thompson had felt otherwise, and so Caryl knew she must somehow ask the Lord for the strength to continue. A decade earlier, when she had first accepted the calling, she had told the Lord that she would serve until He released her, regardless of how tough things became. And so, in an effort to be obedient to that commitment, she asked President Thompson for a special blessing. At that time she was blessed with health and with the ability to carry on her work until the Lord directed her release through the stake presidency.

As Byron reflected on his wife's courage, he remembered how difficult the following three months were, when she struggled to know why she was still serving in such a demanding position. Then one Sunday, when their son-in-law, Michael, was speaking in a sacrament service, the answer came. Byron remembered the words Mike spoke, as though they had just been spoken.

"Brothers and sisters," Mike began, "I need to say some things about Caryl Mackay. Here is a girl who married at age eighteen to the sharpest guy in Granger. They move into their own little home following the wedding. Everything in life looks like roses. They've got it made. Byron is strong. In fact, at Winder Dairy, they still talk about his strength. I work there, and I hear about the feats he did while there. Yes, they have it made until after their first child is born. At that time, Byron becomes desperately ill. All of his joints swelled, making their future very bleak.

"Well, this Caryl Mackay could have decided not to have any more children, that one child and a sick husband were enough. But she and Byron decided to have all the children God would send to them, and I'm glad. I met my wife because of this decision. They had four children, in all, and Caryl provided them with all of the dancing, piano, and swimming lessons they wanted.

"And not only that, but Caryl decided that her problems at home, with her husband's growing dependency and the needs of her children, would not prevent her from serving in whatever capacity the Lord saw fit. And so she has served, and in spite of her great trials, continues to serve the sisters in this stake as their Relief Society president."

As Mike spoke, Byron glanced over at Caryl and saw how visibly touched she was. She had received her answer, and knew that the Lord desired her to continue to serve because He could still use her as a means to reach the women of the stake.

And so Caryl had continued to serve, and Byron had encouraged her, even though his pain and discomfort increased. Then, three months later, she became ill with pneumonia. It was during that time that she had an experience on the night of June 24th, that was one of the most profound messages from the Lord that she had ever received. Although she was coughing constantly and her mind was a total blur, she heard the following message, as clear as though someone was actually speaking to her. "Have Byron call Doctor Elledge at St Mark's Hospital. He is to take you to the emergency room. Your trip to Nauvoo with the Relief Society sisters is not in the plan. You will be blessed because of your faithful service, but you now have your release as president. It is also time for you to undergo open heart surgery, to have your heart repaired. The doctors will know how to proceed."

And so, as Caryl gave Byron instructions, he helped her into the car and drove her immediately to the emergency room at St. Mark's.

Caryl was in the hospital for almost two weeks, and at times wondered if she would make it. She had been connected to a breathing machine and had an I.V. in her arm to assist in getting her nutrients. Doctor Elledge had informed her when the fluids began to leave her lungs that she had been gravely ill when she had been admitted. Tests showed defects in her heart's mitral-valve, and she knew that surgery was imminent.

As Byron thought of how the events had unfolded, he recalled bringing her home from the hospital so that she could gather strength before the operation.

Just four days after returning from the hospital, their son, Dan, and his sweetheart, Debby, were married in the Salt Lake Temple. As he had promised, Ned Winder performed the ceremony. Byron was grateful to be able to sit as a witness and to see Caryl sitting next to their second son, Dan. Glen, their eldest, was also there, as were Peggy and Mike. Sandra had not been to the temple, so stayed in the waiting room until the ceremony was completed.

Byron remembered with fondness how the entire family had gathered outside the temple for pictures. He remembered that evening, sitting with Caryl on two stools, somehow enduring the long, yet enjoyable reception.

Byron smiled as the memories unfolded before him, recalling the Sunday just two weeks after Dan's wedding when Sandra brought a handsome young man, Lane

Henslee, to dinner. He could tell that she was smitten by this young man, and was not surprised when they were married on December 19th, again in the Salt Lake Temple, by Ned Winder.

But, back to Caryl. She had shared her spiritual experience with President Thompson, and the two of them agreed that it was time for her release. The release took place on August 7th, three days after Caryl had re-entered the hospital for a pre-surgery heart catherization. This procedure involved inserting a tube into her arm and extending it into her heart to take pictures of the valves and to plan how the surgery should proceed. But she was only in the hosptal for one night, and so was able to attend Stake Conference for her release.

That had been a beautiful day, as Byron recalled, and never had he been so proud of Caryl. She had served so faithfully and had assisted literally hundreds of sisters over the years of her service. Byron felt humbled to have been given such a Christ-like servant to spend his life with. If only she would be patient as he continued to weed out his imperfections so they could continue on and spend eternity together!

"I can tell you're awake, Byron, because of the smile on your face. Either that or you're having an awfully fun dream."

Byron opened his eyes, again to see Caryl sitting on the sofa to his left.

"Oh, hi, Little Susy. I was just dreaming of having you pull me through the pearly gates, seeing how you're next to being perfect."

"Don't be silly, Byron. I half expect to come in here some time and find you floating in the air on your way to being translated."

The two of them laughed quietly, each enjoying the habit they had formed of always building up the other. It had been a good habit, too, and had allowed them to appreciate and understand one another at a level unfamiliar to many of the marriages they knew. Byron was thankful for that and for the way Caryl lifted his spirits whenever she entered the room.

"Actually, Caryl, I was just thinking back on your release from the Relief Society and all that you went through with your heart."

"Honestly, Byron, I still have a hard time believing that I survived open-heart surgery. But you married me because I vowed to love you with all my heart, and I just hadn't been able to live up to that commitment."

"How about now?" Byron questioned, smiling. "Did that repair job give you an increased capacity to love me?"

"Oh, it did that, alright. I just wish you could love me as much as I love you."

"Well," Byron added, enjoying the exchange, "now, if I recall, my heart is quite a bit bigger than yours, so that should speak for itself."

Caryl reached over and took Byron's hand, then leaned back and closed her eyes. Byron watched with fascination as his beloved sweetheart then relaxed her grasp and quietly fell asleep. He could watch her for hours, thinking that he would never tire of looking at her face and her beautiful blonde hair. She was his angel, and if he ever did make it to the Celestial Kingdom, it would certainly be because of her.

Then, just as quickly as Caryl had escaped into the world of dreams, Byron began to breathe heavier. He, too, fell fast asleep. Neither heard the soft voices from the TV; both were far off in a place where dreams come true. Dreams that, in some strange way, would sustain them through the unexpected events of the months ahead.

· SIX ·
THE BIONIC BISHOP

But the Lord said unto Samuel, Look not on his countenance, or on the height of his stature; because I have refused him: for the Lord seeth not as man seeth; for man looketh on the outward appearance, but the Lord looketh on the heart. 1 Samuel 16:7

June 1, 1980

As Byron and Caryl climbed into their new eight-year-old Plymouth, their stomachs churned with anxiety. They had been called to meet with the stake presidency, and they had no idea what it was about. Byron had been serving as High Priest Group Leader since the previous June, and even though it had not been easy for him to get around, he had felt that he and his assistants had served to their capacity. And so why the meeting? He knew that Caryl wasn't well enough to receive a major calling, and he felt that he could continue to serve, even though it was not easy.

As they pulled into the parking lot at the stake center, Byron turned off the engine, and together they offered a quiet prayer. Byron was the voice, and after taking Caryl's hand in his, he began.

"Heavenly Father, we're so thankful for all of our blessings and for the opportunity you've always given us to serve. We know that at times we've not done as much as we could have, but we have tried, and we thank you for giving us the strength to do so.

"Now, Father, we're not sure what awaits us this evening, but we again commit to doing anything you see fit. We're thankful for the blessing of adversity in our lives, and we truly hope that we are responding as you would have us do. Help us to be uncomplaining in our trials, and help us to be happy and to always reach out to those in need of our love and assistance.

"And Heavenly Father, thank you for giving us such wonderful children—all four of them—and for their companions and their children. We could never be more blessed as a family, and we're especially thankful that Peggy and Mike have been able to build a home behind ours, and that we can be near them at this time in our lives. We wish the others could be closer as well, but we know they are where they are needed, and so we thank thee for thy watchful care over them."

"Now, Father, help us to have Thy Holy Spirit with us as we meet with President Thompson and with his great counselors, Darwin Wahlquist and Bud Rich . . . ."

Closing the prayer and giving each other an affectionate kiss, they left the car and walked into the stake offices. Minutes later, they were sitting in President Thompson's office.

"Byron," President Thompson began, "as a stake presidency, we assume that you're fully worthy of the temple recommend you have in your wallet."

Knowing that President Thompson was waiting for an answer, Byron swallowed anxiously, unable to speak. His nerves were not handling the conversation very well, and it had only begun. But, taking a deep breath, he feebly smiled and nodded affirmatively.

Continuing, President Thompson said, "We're going to divide the 24th Ward and create a new 26th Ward. We've received permission to do so from the First Presidency, and they have approved our recommendation that you serve as bishop of the new ward."

Byron was stunned, feeling like a giant fist had hit him squarely in the stomach. Finally, somewhat regaining his composure, he whispered, "President, I can't even walk up stairs on my own. How can I possibly serve the needs of an entire ward?"

"Byron, here is a letter signed by President Kimball, authorizing us to call you as bishop. Do you want to turn him down?"

"No, I don't, but I still can't imagine him calling me, in my condition, to be a bishop."

"You'll do just fine, Byron. Now, go home and prayerfully consider who you would like to have as your counselors. The Lord will make these names known to you."

Several minutes later, after completing the interview, Byron and Caryl drove north on Redwood Road in silence.

Finally, Byron spoke. "Caryl, this has to be a call from the Lord, because no one else would think that someone with my disabilities could serve as a bishop. I feel that the only way I'll be able to do this is by calling our son-in-law, Michael, as my first counselor, and Dennis Paxman as second counselor. They are very spiritual young men and hard workers."

"I think they would be marvelous counselors, Byron, and I'll be surprised if the Lord doesn't give you confirmation on both when you pray about them."

"You know, Caryl," Byron continued, "prayer really is my passport to spiritual power. I've not always known that, but with what we've been through, I have as strong a testimony of that as I do that the Church is true."

For the next several days, Byron fasted periodically and prayed fervently that he would have the strength to fulfill such a strenuous and pivotal Church calling. He had heard Elder Neal A. Maxwell once say that the entire Church revolved around the bishop, that the office of bishop was the most crucial of all Church callings. And Byron could see why, as the bishops he had known were men of God who selflessly labored for hours on end, impacting and literally changing lives. These thoughts repeatedly entered Byron's mind, and each time they did, he prayed for forgiveness of his sins and for the ability to measure up to the Lord's expectations.

As he had anticipated, Byron did receive a confirmation that Michael and Dennis should be his counselors. He notified the stake president of those choices, as well as that he felt prompted to choose Dennis Wilson as his executive secretary and Rod Ashworth as his ward clerk. These were marvelous men, and he knew that if he was to succeed, it would be through their dedication and skill.

The week passed quickly, and finally the next Sunday, June 8th, arrived. As Byron's name was being presented, he questioned for a brief moment whether he would receive a unanimous sustaining vote from his new ward members. His fears were unfounded, however, as all hands expressed confidence and support of him as their new bishop.

The rest of the meeting was a blur for Byron, although he did remember struggling to his feet and the arduous task of planting one foot in front of the other as he made his way to the podium to speak. He knew that alone he could never succeed in such a calling, and that yet, with the help of the Lord, he would somehow accomplish the task at hand.

Following the meeting, Byron received a confirmation that he would be able to perform the job of a bishop as President Thompson blessed him with strength and power beyond his own abilities. When his ordination was finished,

Byron looked up and immediately gazed into Caryl's eyes. His vision was blurred by tears, however, and he was unable to see that she, too, was overcome by the significance of what had just taken place.

Arising, Byron expressed appreciation to those assisting, and then slowly walked over to Caryl. He embraced her and then each of the children as he had never done before. They were the most blessed of families, and at that moment he wouldn't have traded places with anyone else in the entire world.

Later that evening, after the other members of the bishopric had gone home, Byron sat quietly in the bishop's office, considering the weight of responsibility that now rested squarely upon his shoulders. The power of what he had experienced that day had touched him in a way he would not have thought possible. Never in his life had he felt such a change come over him. President Thompson had told him that the only feeling comparable to being ordained a bishop was the feeling of emptiness that accompanied the release from the same office. He certainly understood the first of these emotions, and if the latter of the two events was as profound, then he never wanted to see that day arrive.

As he sat there, cupping his crippled hands on the desk before him, Byron marveled that the Lord would accept such hands to perform His work. For the first time, Byron realized that his "spirit hands" were not gnarled and crippled, but were seasoned with service—both in his profession as a barber and in his labors in the kingdom.

Byron was humbled to think that all of the surgeries of the past decade had served to sustain his body in preparation for this calling. He had long before determined to never complain, but to face each adversity with faith.

"Thank you, Heavenly Father," he suddenly whispered out loud, surprising himself. "I have always tried to have a grateful heart, Father, for being loved by you enough to be blessed with these physical problems. I know they have been for my good, and that even though the refiner's fire has been uncomfortably hot at times, still I am thankful for the years of preparation that have brought me to this sacred calling."

Opening his eyes, Byron retrieved his copy of the scriptures, and turned slowly to Ether in the Book of Mormon. He was appreciative of the years Moroni had spent in condensing the Jaredite records and of the insight shared in Chapter 12, verse 27. Quietly, yet audibly, he read the words that Christ had long ago spoken to Moroni:

"And if men come unto me I will show unto them their weakness. I give unto men weakness that they may be humble; and my grace is sufficient for all men that humble themselves before me; for if they humble themselves before me, and have faith in me, then will I make weak things become strong unto them."

If the Savior's words were true, Byron reasoned, then perhaps his physical deformities were given to him so that he could be humble enough for the atonement to affect his life. The principle of grace was little understood, and yet if he grasped the concept correctly, he knew that, far beyond his energies or his works, the grace of God would allow him to inherit the Celestial Kingdom with the righteous members of his family.

"I will make weak things become strong unto them," he read again, focusing once more on his physical disaibilities. At that moment, the idea occurred to Byron that he should exert himself physically by going into the members' homes as often as possible. In addition, he and his counselors would invite the ward members to his office to extend calls to them. Hopefully, when the individuals realized the dedication with which the bishopric would serve, they would accept and serve with equal dedication.

As these thoughts flooded Byron's mind, he made another decision. He and his counselors would join together in setting apart each person called, and this blessing would be given within the sacred walls of the bishop's office. Byron couldn't really explain it to himself, but there was something different about the office in which he now sat, and he would take advantage of that difference in blessing lives.

Concluding the prayer that he had earlier begun, Byron then asked the Lord to bring into his mind the names of individuals who had special needs so that he could attend to those needs.

Moments later, as he exited the church parking lot and drove home, Byron thought of Sister Ann Carton, whose husband, Willis, or "Willie", was a non-member. Ann was a very special lady, and she truly loved her husband. Byron also knew that Willie smoked a great deal and was in poor health as a result. If only Willie could feel loved, Byron reasoned, his habits would change and he would be ready for baptism.

As Byron thought of Willie and of making an impact on the lives of those in the ward, his mind was flooded with new perceptions and thoughts. Even though he was limited physically, he knew that perhaps he could use his handicaps to his advantage to serve as an example of an uncomplaining servant of the Lord.

Later that night, as he and Caryl nestled in each other's arms, Byron was the first to speak. "You know, Little Susy, I have never had a day like today. I don't really know how to explain my emotions, but it is almost like I'm a new person just serving as bishop in Byron Mackay's worn out old body."

"You'll be so effective, Byron, because you live so close to the Spirit. I can't wait to see how the Lord works through you and performs his miracles! I just couldn't be more proud of you than I am right now."

"Well, you're the reason I'm serving, I can tell you that. "Say," Byron continued, smiling, "do you remember the time we went fishing up at Currant Creek? Wally Beckstead carried me down the steep slope to the river so that I could fish. You brought the folding chair I sat in, and even though I could cast out, I needed Sandra to reel the line back in. Anyway, I remember how proud Sandra was, bringing those fish in for me. She seemed to be happiest when she was serving."

"And what you're saying, Byron, is that even though you didn't ever think you would be called as bishop, you'll be happier than ever before just because you're serving."

"Well, yes, I suppose I will. But that isn't what I was thinking. I was actually reflecting on how happy Wally and Sandra were, helping me. If I can convey the joy that comes through service, then our new ward will really jell, and the Lord will be pleased with us."

"Just don't wear yourself out, Byron. That's all I ask."

"Good heavens, Caryl, I'm already worn out! When I got home tonight, I felt like I was walking on two broken ankles. So, I can't wear out in the service of the Lord. But I can wear a few others out as they carry me around and see that I get to where I'm supposed to be. Sounds kinda fun, wouldn't you agree?!"

Both laughed, hugged each other even tighter, and before long were fast asleep. It had been a long day for them, and yet in ways they had not thought possible, it had also been their happiest.

The weeks passed, and with their passing came increased understanding. Those that Byron surrounded himself with were even more capable than he had imagined, and never once did anyone turn down a calling to serve. And each calling was unique, too. For instance, in calling Sister Barbara Ormsbee as the new Primary President, all three members of the bishopric were present to make the call. After it had been extended, Barbara said, "Actually, brethren, I don't have to take time to ask the Lord if this calling is right for me because I have known of it for the past two weeks. I don't say this immodestly, but I felt this call was coming, so I am prepared to serve."

This experience, like so many others, was humbling for Byron and his counselors. They felt more and more indebted to the Lord for the direction they were receiving. Byron knew they would make mistakes, and so he determined to keep the commandments more faithfully than he ever had before. Righteousness really did open the windows of heaven, and to make correct decisions, Byron truly needed to be in tune with the Holy Spirit.

One evening Byron found himself visiting at LDS Hospital with his non-member friend, Willie Carton, who had just experienced a heart attack. At that time, Byron remembered an event that had occurred years earlier with his son, Dan.

"Willie, you've met Dan, haven't you?"

"You mean your son, Dan?"

Nodding affirmatively, Byron continued. "Well, Dan's twenty-five years old now, has served a mission to Brazil, married Debby two years ago, and is getting ready to graduate from the Y. But twelve years ago, when he was a 13-year-old scout, he and I had quite an experience that I'd like to share with you."

Smiling, Willie silently nodded, enjoying this unusual man who was always so cheerful and full of stories.

"Well," Byron recalled, "the scout troop Dan belonged to decided to make their own kayaks and test them out in the Snake River in Idaho. Dan and I worked hard, cutting out the wood and bending the ribs around the bulkheads. Finally, we put the canvas skin on, stretching it tightly over the frame. While Dan was painting it, I suggested that we name it Arapidaparatus."

Realizing that Willie didn't understand the name, Byron explained further. "You know, A-rapid-apparatus. Dan thought this was some kind of Indian name until I said it slowly to him. Well, we both felt good about the name, and so we painted it on both sides of the kayak."

"Did the kayak work, Byron?" Willie pressed, anxious to know the outcome of the story.

"Oh, it worked alright! Actually, it was a fairly big boat for someone Dan's size, so I inflated some inner tubes and stuck them in each end just in case the kayak capsized. That way I figured Dan had a fighting chance, since the boat would stay on top of the water."

Sensing that he had the man's attention, Byron smiled and continued with his story. "Well, Willie, the kayak worked nicely on the first run down the river, and Dan was pretty proud of what we had built. But during his second run, he nearly lost his kayak *and* his life in some unexpectedly rough water. Someone had cut down a large tree, and it was partially submerged in the fast moving water. When Dan struck it, he frantically grabbed onto some branches and watched as his kayak was sucked under, cracking and ripping as the water forced limbs through the canvas. The boat ribs snapped as it disappeared, and for several hours they thought they had lost it. But with 12 scouts and two scoutmasters working, they finally pried it out from under the tree in the middle of the river. When it finally came out, it literally shot to the surface, the inner tubes still full of air. Dan was able to finish his ride, floating down the rest of the river in his wrecked kayak. Needless to say, Dan was a hero among the boys for having had the foresight to insert the inner tubes to keep it afloat."

"That's quite a story, Byron, but I have a hunch you're not finished." Smiling at the bishop who had befriended him, Willie motioned for Byron to continue.

"Well, you're right, Willie . . . I'm not finished. Actually, I was going to draw an analogy. You see, in a way, I'm an inner tube that the Lord has inserted in your kayak. He knows how treacherous the waters are in this life, and I've been sent to help keep you afloat. Now, I know you've suffered a major heart attack and that you're living on borrowed time. What I don't know is how long you're going to keep swimming around down here on earth's water."

"Nor do I, Byron, although I wish I did. I know what you're getting at, and I just don't know if I have the strength to give up cigarettes and to live my life as a Latter-day Saint. It just seems too hard for me to even consider."

"Well, I appreciate your thinking, Willie; and even though I've never used tobacco, I have my own faults to overcome, so I understand your lack of confidence. But you can do it, Willy, and if I'm not mistaken, one day the Lord will be using you in much the same manner as he is using me, helping to put air in other people's kayaks."

Both men laughed; and then, clearing his throat, Byron concluded, "Now, Willie, if I'm not mistaken, your daughter, Beth, is seven years old now and will turn eight this coming December. I think it would be marvelous if you were to make it your quest to find out that the Church is true. You know the Lord won't deceive you, but will guide your thoughts as you sincerely ask him. But there's a catch, Willie, that I'm sure you're already aware of."

"And that's my cigarettes, right?"

"See how perceptive you are, Willie? But my counselors and I will give you a priesthood blessing, and with our faith and yours, you'll be able to throw those coffin nails away once and for all!"

Again both men laughed. Then, sensing it was time to leave, Byron extended his hand to his friend and then slowly worked his way to his feet. Shuffling slowly toward the door, he looked back and said, "Think about what I've said Willie, and I'll be back to visit you in a couple of days."

"I will, Bishop, but I don't want you to get your hopes up."

"It's the Lord's hopes I'm concerned with, Willie . . . His and your family's. But then you're a truth seeker, so you'll know, I'm sure of it."

Long after Byron had left, Willis Carton stared at the ceiling, his mind reeling. Who was this man—this cripple—who could come into his life and make the impression that he had? And what about this thing the Mormons called "inspiration?" Was Byron inspired to say what he had about his giving up tobacco and baptizing his little Beth? It all seemed so impossible and yet so clearly laid out before him.

For Bishop Byron Mackay, the weeks of service turned into months, and with each passing day, new challenges presented themselves. Between his work at the barber shop and his responsibilities as bishop, he found that he had less and less time to spend with his family. Even so, and in spite of his physical problems, he and Caryl had never been happier. They knew that this was a moment in time when they must learn to rely upon the Lord to sustain them, and in this they were not disappointed.

Summer came, and before Byron knew it, he and his ward youth were traveling north to Idaho and then into Yellowstone Park for a youth conference. When they arrived at the Shurtliff cabin in Island Park, the youth and adults alike were thrilled to have Byron and the other members of their bishopric with them. Byron was the life of the party, laughing and joking, even at his own expense.

One of Byron's favorite jokes surfaced after the group leaders met for a planning session inside the cabin. As he shook hands with Kristin Ashworth, the Young Women's President, he pulled his hand up to eye level and exclaimed, "Now, Kristin, look what you did to my hand!" He winked at her, she smiled back, and the others in the room giggled out of endearment for their bishop. He always had a one liner to put others at ease about his physical impairments, and they appreciated his lighthearted approach to the difficulties he lived with.

On the second evening in Island Park, the youth surprised Byron by presenting him with a t-shirt with the words BIONIC BISHOP inscribed on the front. They were well aware of Byron's physical limitations and of the many artificial body parts that had been inserted into his frame. They wanted him to know that, in their minds, there was nothing he couldn't accomplish!

One of the activities of the conference involved descending into the steep and treacherous Firehole Canyon to enjoy a swimming party in a swimming hole. Byron knew he couldn't walk into the canyon, which frustrated him because he truly wanted to spend his time with the young men and women.

While considering this dilemma, two of the leaders, Jim Johnson and Scott Shurtliff, made a seat with their arms and lifted Byron down the mountain in perfect comfort. They placed him on a rock, and for hours he and Caryl yelled and laughed at the kids, who were swimming and frolicking in the water around them. At the conclusion of this activity, the "chariot" arrived back at the rock, and the same brethren carried him back up out of the canyon in preparation for the evening activities.

It seemed as though there was nothing the ward members wouldn't do for Byron, and this loyalty spread throughout the ward. In addition to the growth and unity brought about by the youth conference, other, more unnoticed miracles also took place.

One couple, Marilyn and Rick Beard, had not been able to bear children. Learning of this, Byron gave Marilyn a blessing, informing her that the Lord would bless her with children. She soon found that she was expecting, and before long a son was born to her and Rick. Still, further lessons were to be learned as their baby, whom they named Conley, had been born with a defective heart. Within a short time he quietly passed away, again leaving the Beards without children. Since that time, however, five additional children were born to them, fulfilling Byron's blessing.

Another sister, Rayleen Barnes, was tragically involved in an automobile accident. Through Byron's energies, the ward members rallied around her and added their faith and prayers for her recovery. These prayers were answered, and Byron was deeply humbled to have played a small part in this miracle.

Yet another sister, Susan Werner, had a different outcome to her difficulties. She gave birth to a beautiful baby boy, only to find that she had developed a heart condition from the complications of the birth. She soon lapsed into a coma, and again the ward members were called upon to fast and pray in her behalf.

Stake Conference took place at this critical time, and the visiting authority, Elder Loren C. Dunn, was called upon to give Susan a blessing. He blessed her that she would soon be restored to her perfect health and strength.

Although the doctors attending to Susan doubted that she would ever come out of the coma, one evening she awakened and began speaking to those attending her. Not many minutes later, Byron and Caryl entered her hospital room just to be with her and give her comfort. Taking Byron's hand in hers, Susan looked up into his eyes, and whispered, "I love you, Bishop." Byron was overwhelmed with Christ-like love and compassion, and as he left the hospital to attend a meeting, he sensed that he was learning lessons that he would carry with him into the eternities.

Susan's words to Byron were her last. After the Mackays' brief visit, her tired heart stopped beating. Her husband, Tom, was with her at the time of her passing, and he immediately phoned Byron, who at that moment was conducting a bishopric meeting. Byron and his counselors immediately concluded the meeting, shortly thereafter arriving at the hospital.

After embracing Tom and offering their condolences, Tom returned to his wife's side. Running his fingers through her hair, he quietly whispered, "When I see Susan again, I'm going to get after her for leaving me like this."

The ward referred to the Werners' ordeal as "Sue's 100 Days." Byron shared his thoughts with them when they met at the chapel to conclude their fast for Susan, for Rayleen, and for the Beards. The Lord had intervened in behalf of these people as directed in Section 42 of the Doctrine and Covenants. Each had received priesthood blessings, and each had submitted to the Lord's will. With increased understanding, Byron taught that Elder Dunn's blessing to Susan had indeed been fulfilled, although not in the manner they had anticipated. She no longer lay in a coma, but was restored to her perfect health and strength in the Spirit World. This was a miracle not to be forgotten.

On one occasion, Kristin Ashworth, who was serving as the Young Women's President, remarked to the youth that "Bishop Mackay has a magic about him. Like King Arthur, under Bishop Mackay's leadership, the 26th ward has become a Camelot. It is filled with love, hope, and never-ending optimism."

As 1981 progressed, Byron found himself visiting again and again with Willie Carton, encouraging him to keep the commandments so that he could learn for himself that the Church was true. Willie finally received this testimony, and just before Christmas his son, Kelly, led him into the waters of baptism while Byron and other ward members looked on.

Following Willie's confirmation and ordination to the office of priest in the Aaronic Priesthood, he re-entered the baptismal waters and there used his priesthood for the very first time, baptizing his daughter, Beth. He knew that he would have never enjoyed that moment, had Byron left him alone and not befriended him. Little did Willie know as he became a member of the Lord's Church, that in just four short years he would be called upon to serve the 26th Ward as their bishop. But for now, without knowing of his future, Willie looked to Byron for support, drinking freely from the fountain of love and courage that Byron so humbly provided.

As 1982 arrived, Byron found himself in surprisingly good health. His artificial knees and hips were holding up well, and he honestly felt that his arthritis was not progressing. Wally Beckstead had replaced Frank Robinson as Byron's assistant in the barber shop, and Byron appreciated his help there. By this time, Byron's hands were totally deformed, making it difficult to cut hair. Even so, he would invite his customers to slide down in the chair, and somehow he had the strength to continue to provide for himself and Caryl. By now, the kids were married—each in the temple—and he was thrilled with being a grandpa and playing with his newest family members.

On January 10th, Byron recorded the following entry in his journal:

> It's been almost a year since I last wrote in this journal. I have had some good experiences as Bishop. By now I have come to love the members of our ward so much for being so nice to me. They really look out for me, and are so obedient. I guess that's one thing that's so hard to get used to—people respecting me for my calling.
>
> My health keeps surprising me. I know it is through the help of the Lord that I'm able to just keep going.

What Byron did not know was that the coming summer would bring with it a new challenge for his body. First, his right hand began to lose its feeling and to become immobile. As a result, on the 26th of October, he had it operated on.

The joints in his right thumb were fused together, and he was given "new" knuckles in his other fingers.

This operation was followed with another just three weeks later. This time, the joints in his left thumb were fused together, and once again he received new, artificial knuckles.

Returning home to convalesce, Byron thought that before long he would be back at work, cutting hair. What he didn't know was that a month later, at 6:30 in the morning on December 12th, he would suffer a major seizure. When he awakened from this nightmare, he found that the paramedics had transported him to St. Mark's Hospital and that he was listed in serious condition.

Again, prayers were offered and faith was exercised. The ward members rallied around their bishop, and before long he was resting comfortably at home, enjoying Christmas with his family.

Although 1983 began routinely, for Byron it commenced a period of frustration and discomfort. His words were barely legible in his journal as he painfully penned the following:

> My handwriting is not very good . . . [and from my surgery] my right hand is still very numb and very weak. I sure want to write about the nice Christmas we have just had. I want to say how good my family members have been to me through my troubles. Three weeks ago today I had my seizure, but I've been administered to, and I believe I'll get better so I can go back and run my barber shop. I want to get my arms and hands better so I can work for a few more years. The Lord has been so good to us, as the money just seems to come from everywhere so we can pay our bills. I haven't worked for two months.

Yes, the year had begun calmly, with Byron and Caryl learning to rely upon the Lord for quiet miracles to sustain them. Little did they know that lessons of a different nature were about to be taught. Changes of immense proportion were gathering force, preparing to impact and even further alter their lives.

• SEVEN •
REACHING OUT

If thou art called to pass through tribulation . . . he Son of Man hath descended below them all. Art thou greater than he? . . . Hold on thy way, and the priesthood shall remain with thee. . . . Thy days are known, and thy years shall not be numbered less.
D&C 122:5, 8-9

Sunday Morning — January 26, 1983

The sky was overcast with a bitter west wind as Byron shuffled out to his car with Caryl at his side.

"I don't know," he whispered, a feeling of emptiness seeming to envelope him. "I just haven't had enough time . . ."

"Oh, Byron, you can't say that. Why, you've done more good in these three years than you could ever imagine."

"But, I'm just getting the hang of things, Caryl. If the Lord could just sustain me a little while longer, I could . . ."

"There you go again, Bishop Mackay, telling the Lord how to run his Church!"

Byron glanced over at Caryl, who was now sitting in the driver's seat, ready to leave for church. She radiated such beauty, and always seemed to have just the right words to say to him.

"You're right, honey, as always. I just wish for selfish things, I guess, although the Lord knows my desire is simply to serve him."

An hour later, after being released as bishop, Byron gazed out into the congregation and fought back the tears. How could he ever have been so blessed? The good Lord had never assembled a finer group of people, and he would forever be in His debt for what being their bishop had added to his life. He knew that his health precluded him from serving longer, as his hands were so crippled that he couldn't even hold a pen to sign baptismal and temple recommends.

Still, as he sat there, having had the mantle removed from his shoulders, Byron grimaced in pain. The words spoken three years earlier by President Thompson were ringing loudly in his ears. "The only feeling comparable to being ordained a bishop is the feeling of emptiness that accompanies being released from the same office." That emptiness was real for Byron, and he just hoped that he could continue to serve the people in the ward, regardless of the capacity. As he considered the possibility of having a "normal" calling again, his mind reflected on the words of Elder Bruce R. McConkie that he had read in the second to last chapter of *The Promised Messiah*. In the chapter titled, "Seek the Face of the Lord Always," Byron remembered reading these words: "The Lord loves people, not office holders." While he had held the most sacred office of bishop, he must direct his energy to whatever calling that might be extended to him. Regardless of whether he was asked to serve in a Primary calling, to work in the resource center, or whatever, he would do his very best to fulfill the work honorably. He just hoped that he would be given a job, and not be given a rest from church service.

Almost two months later, as Byron settled again into the

routine of cutting hair and caring for his fragile physical health, he had an experience that was both frightening and insightful. It occurred early one morning as he awakened in pain. In his journal, he recorded:

> I had a very different experience, lying in bed at about 2:00 A.M. I felt the devil, or one of his angels, come into our bedroom and stand at the foot of the bed. He immediately brought his power onto me, so that I felt something like a strong electrical vibration taking control of my entire body, so much so that I couldn't move. It seemed as though my feet were almost to the ceiling and my head down on the bed. I felt like my heart could no longer beat because of so much electricity. I commanded Satan to leave by the power of the Melchizedek Priesthood and in the name of Jesus Christ. As soon as I had said this I went limp and was relaxed so that I could see with my spiritual eyes [this] man walk out of the bedroom. I bear testimony of this in Christ's name, Amen.

As Byron shared this experience with Caryl, they concluded that the Lord had allowed him to have it so that he would understand two things. The first was that Satan was real, and not an imaginary force, and that he, or his host of spirits, were empowered to afflict the children of men. The second was that the Savior would, or could, help him out of any problem, regardless of how difficult. They reasoned that just as the Lord had cut him loose from the power of the Adversary, so too could the Lord cut him loose from his physical afflictions so that he could provide for his family.

And Byron did provide for his family. But his barbering was very limited, and so he was blessed to have Keith Brower come into his shop and assume the primary haircutting responsibilities. Keith was an excellent barber, and Byron's customers seemed to love the spirit of optimism and happiness that always radiated within the walls of Byron's barber shop.

Even so, optimism was not something that continued for Byron, personally. His paralysis continued to increase, and soon he found himself in the hospital, having his spine operated on.

A month after this surgery, with the feeling returning to his body, Byron's right elbow and shoulder began to constantly ache. Upon visiting with Dr. Dunn, an orthopedic surgeon at the University of Utah Medical Center, Byron learned that nothing could be done to alleviate the pain. He was told that his body was simply wearing out and that he would need to learn to simply tolerate the pain and discomfort. As a result of this diagnosis, Byron was given state disability, effectively reducing his barbering to a part-time status.

As if these problems weren't enough, when summer arrived, Byron fell and broke several ribs. His body was deteriorating, and there was nothing he could do about it. Still, he kept up his spirits, and whenever friends and family members came to see him he would laugh and joke with them. He continued to teach principles of the gospel to whomever he met, encouraging them to keep the commandments and live each day as though it were their last.

As Thanksgiving came and passed, Byron learned from his doctors that cancer had been diagnosed on his right eyelid. Surgery was scheduled, and on December first, while most of the world was beginning the Christmas season with celebration, Byron found himself on the operating table. After a five-hour ordeal, the surgeons had removed the lower eyelid and reconstructed it the best they could.

The highlight of the year, for Byron, took place six days before Christmas. With Caryl and all of their family members in attendance, Byron was surprised to receive an early Christmas present.

"Well, Dad," Peggy exclaimed, "at the first of this year, I presented the family with the idea of surprising you this Christmas with your very first new car. So, here it is!"

Excitedly, Glen spoke up. "I know how you love cars, Dad, beginning back when you courted Mom in your '34 Ford. My earliest memory is of riding in that car with you, standing on the seat with my arm around you . . ."

"Get on with it, Glen," Peggy pressed. "The kids are starved."

"That's okay," Caryl added, wondering if brothers and sisters ever stopped acting like brothers and sisters. "Your father has always loved cars and has washed his at least once every week on Saturday nights."

"I remember," Sandra chimed in, "how you used to take me to the car wash, and let me help you dry the water off and shine up your car for Sunday."

"Well, kids, I appreciate all of your memories," Byron interrupted, laughing anxiously. "But, I can tell something's up, so why don't you just throw the words out, Glen, and we'll see where they land."

The family laughed, once again enjoying Byron's ever-present sense of humor.

"Okay, Dad," Glen continued, clearing his throat. "We just want you to know that we've been saving our sheckles all year long and that the shiny new car outside is yours . . . that is, unless you want to give it to me!"

"My land!" Byron exclaimed excitedly as he was helped to his feet to look out the window. "What on . . .? I don't know what to say, I . . ."

"Just say how excited you are," Dan added. "It's a new Oldsmobile Ciera Brougham, and it's itching for you and Mom to take a ride."

Looking outside, Byron indeed found himself gazing at a shiny maroon Oldsmobile—his very first new car! As he wiped the tears from his eyes, he could barely make out the images of his family clustering around him. He wasn't sure, but he thought he saw their moistened eyes through his own tears. He was overwhelmed to think that his life's dream of driving a new car had at last come true. But even more, he was touched by the outpouring of love that came from his family. Why, he was the luckiest man in all of Granger! How could he ever repay the Lord for enriching his life as He had done? It just wasn't possible.

A few moments later, after being helped into the car by his sons, Byron glanced over at Caryl, who was sitting in the driver's seat, starting the engine.

"Well, Little Susy," he smiled, waving at his family as they stood on the sidewalk to his right, "let's go for a ride. I haven't felt this good in years!"

"I hope we don't crash," Caryl whispered, looking anxiously at the traffic as she approached the curb. "After all, Byron, I wouldn't want anything bad to happen to you!"

The two chuckled quietly, the motor purred softly, and soon the shiny new Oldsmobile was a tiny speck in the distance. One by one, the children and grandchildren turned and filed back into the house. After all, dinner was long overdue, and no one had any idea when they would see Byron and Caryl again.

1984 arrived, and with record snowfall came daily progress. Byron was able to drive his car to work, even though it was some time before he could cut hair for an entire day. Finally, on March 11th, after a hard day at the barber shop, Byron returned home exhausted. He showered and then retired to his favorite recliner in the family room to relax and watch television. As he sat down, a pain shot through his chest, restricting his ability to breathe. The pain finally subsided, but returned again in the middle of the night. The same experience occurred a third time the following morning as Byron was shaving. And so, calling his son-in-law, Mike, and Dick Buckholt, he was immediately administered to. He then went to the doctor's office and learned that he was in the middle of several heart attacks.

These attacks continued into the following week and were accompanied by Caryl having her own heart problems. Realizing that her heart was beating irregularly, she returned to Doctor Ritchie, who told her that her pulse was beating between 150 and 160 times a minute.

The tests for Byron and Caryl seemed endless. Even so, they continued to exercise faith and knew that they were in the Lord's hands.

On April 7th, as a way to express himself to his family, Byron wrote the following letter to them:

There are so many good things to consider, and this life is so good to me and my family that you should know that I wouldn't change it, even if it was possible. If I were to live my life over, I'm sure I would marry my cute little Caryl. I would go through arthritis again for how it became the way that my testimony has become as strong as it has.

I'd have another house without stairs, and have the same children, who Caryl and I have had so much fun and joy with. I would buy another Apache trailer and go camping and fishing, and back to Washington, D.C., New York, Niagara Falls, and of course the Book of Mormon country. I would have a fireplace and hamburgers on Saturday nights. I would still tie the kids' door shut on Christmas Eve and go to Johnson's Ice Cream/Popcorn store, in Sugar House. I'd have buttermilk hot cakes on General Conference mornings.

If I were to live my life again, I would be sure that my kids had cats and dogs and that they married good companions. I'd make believe I was boss around here, and then I would be ready to go back to my Father in Heaven when He wanted me to and wait for my family there.

My love to my family, Dad

Not long after writing this letter, Byron felt the numbness returning again to his entire body. He found that he needed assistance even to walk, and again a living night-mare prevailed.

On June 4th, while celebrating his thirty-sixth wedding anniversary with Caryl, Byron walked into the kitchen to get a drink of water. Suddenly he lurched forward, landing hard on the kitchen floor. Caryl immediately got on the phone and located Fern Hanson. Fern came quickly with her son, Blaine, and they pulled him onto the bed.

When Doctor Lamb was finally able to examine Byron, he determined that three vertebrae needed to be fused in his neck. That hopefully would relieve some of the pressure on his spinal cord.

Learning of the impending surgery, Byron's ward members held a special fast in his behalf, with Bishop Holt, Byron's replacement, coming over with his counselors and giving Byron a blessing. In the blessing, Bishop Holt informed Byron that the Lord still had a mission for him to perform on the earth and that he should be of cheer, allowing the Lord's spirit to pour out, especially to the young people of the ward.

And so, on July 26th, with hope filling Byron's heart, surgery was finally performed. But as Byron awakened, he found that he had lost the use of his legs and arms. Two days later, he was completely paralyzed. The doctors then learned that while the surgery had straightened the three vertebrae, it had now put new pressure on the top vertebrae. This vertebrae was filling with calcium, squeezing his spinal cord, and thus causing the paralysis.

In speaking with Doctor Lamb about his condition, Byron indicated that he would just as soon die as have more surgery. The doctor understood his feelings, but convinced Byron that they had no other choice but to try again.

And so, on the 23rd of August, a second operation took place. The doctors created a larger channel for Byron's spinal cord, hoping that Byron would at least regain partial feeling from his waist up.

Returning home as a quadriplegic, Byron sensed that his life would never be the same again. But still he remembered the priesthood blessing, as well as the sense of peace that Caryl had received through prayer. She had felt that all would be well, and that she would be given insight in caring for Byron. In this she was not disappointed, for, as problems arose that were foreign to her, she would immediately know how to respond and to make Byron's life tolerable.

Keeping her own journal religiously, as Caryl and Byron had committed they would do, Caryl made the following entries:

August 23rd — Byron can breathe and swallow better.

August 25th — Byron has feeling in his little finger.

August 26th — Byron can rub his thumb and index finger together.

September 5 — Byron felt a fly walk on his hand.

September 7 — Byron sneezed 3 times (It has been 3 months since he could do that).

On September 16th, following a family fast, the entire Mackay family surrounded Byron's bed. The sons administered to him, reaffirming that he was going to get better.

Later that evening, the family again gathered around the the recliner Byron was using as a hospital bed. Mike then leaned up against his father's feet and began pushing against him in a commanding manner.

"Come on, Dad," he urged, "you've got to get these legs going so you can begin walking and go fishing next summer!"

"I've tried so many times to do that," Byron answered in frustration, "but nothing happens. I can see my feet and feel like they will move, but there's just no connection between them and my head."

But Mike continued to push, with Byron only feeling his head move back and forth on the pillow, with no sensation below.

Then, suddenly, Byron felt like he was pushing against Mike's hands. Sensing this, Mike said, "Dad, you're pushing me!"

The family was silent, observing the miracle that was unfolding before them. First the right foot moved and then the left. Caryl, ever the cheerleader, exclaimed, "Right, left . . . right, left!"

The grandchildren began clapping, and the adults, including Byron, were crying tears of joy. Prayers had been answered, progress had been made, and Byron was determined that he would walk and resume his activities and responsibilities. Never had the power of prayer been so evident, and with the Lord's blessing, he knew there was nothing he couldn't do.

Before long, Byron felt well enough to be strapped to his wheelchair. He was surrounded by pillows, his head was strapped to a board, Indian-style, and a belt secured him to the chair, preventing him from falling out. This new arrangement allowed his ever-helpful son-in-law, Mike, to come through the back yard each afternoon after work and push Byron outside into the back yard. Byron would then spend hours listening to the birds and enjoying the breeze as it blew the autumn leaves around him. And always, always did Byron have a prayer of gratitude in his heart.

Six weeks later, as he was sitting in his wheelchair in front of the garage, one of Caryl's piano students, eight-year-old Jennifer Holt, came out the front door from having her lesson. She and Byron struck up a conversation, and after exchanging greetings, Jennifer took a deep breath, and said, "Do you know, Bishop Mackay, that without my mother telling me to, I pray for you every night? So does my little brother."

Once again, Byron felt his eyes blur as he swallowed and answered, "Thank you, Jennifer. I surely do appreciate you and your brother's prayers."

Not long after this conversation, Byron was able to stand on his own and take his first step. He then began to slowly walk from room to room, gathering strength with each passing day.

Then one afternoon, again while Jennifer Holt was sitting at the piano for another lesson, Byron passed by, and said, "Well, Jennifer, Heavenly Father has heard your prayers, and here I am walking again."

Without speaking, Jennifer looked at Byron from head to foot and then, looking up into his eyes, broke out in a grin, smiling ear to ear. She then looked over at Caryl, continued to smile, and resumed practicing. She learned a great deal that moment, and it would serve as an anchor for her for years to come.

Time passed, and with each new day Byron became more mobile. His therapy sessions in the pool of water, with a life preserver around his neck, helped the most. And although his legs continued to get tangled up beneath him in the water, the physical therapist was always there to help and give encouragement.

Recording her thoughts at this time, Caryl wrote, "Byron is truly my hero, for through all he has gone through, his courage and faith have shone like a torch, lighting the way for others."

But Byron didn't see himself as a hero. Rather, he just felt thankful to be alive and to share his life with so many caring, loving people.

That fall, Byron returned to the barber shop for three-hour shifts and attended the three-hour block of church meetings. Plagued with spasms throughout his body, his left leg became so dysfunctional that it began to contract to an extreme that Byron felt would break his artificial knee.

This setback made Byron believe that he would never walk again. Even so, his family felt differently. And so, three days after the leg spasm, Caryl and their daughter, Peggy, went to a medical supply store and purchased some attachments for Byron's walker. These held his arms secure and kept him from falling sideways. When Byron became comfortable with the attachments, Glen suggested he swing his arms as he tried to walk without the support. Byron took Glens's suggestion to heart, and with renewed hope and determination, began to walk—first in the living room, and then down the hall. On Christmas evening, after visiting with family members, Byron penned these words:

> This has been a good Christmas. I walked alone today, three times around the room! I love my Father in Heaven. It's unbelievable, getting around inside the house.

It was three months later. After almost a year without driving, Byron climbed into his new Oldsmobile and drove down to his barber shop. While he didn't cut any hair that day, he did enjoy being there for a little while and visiting with those who came in.

Three days later, Byron returned a second time to the shop and was able to cut Peter Thompson's hair. Peter was his stake president, and that night Byron recorded his feelings again in his journal:

> I drove down and cut Pete Thompson's hair today. I made $6.00, which is the first money I've made in about a year. It sure felt good!

Throughout the year and the many adversities facing him, Byron had also served as a counselor in the stake Sunday School presidency. He loved this job, and even though it was not demanding, he felt a sense of belonging, knowing that the Lord was continuing to use him.

While Byron was convalescing, Caryl cared for him, ignoring her own heart problems. She also began to speak to church groups and to represent Byron in giving hope to others.

Two days before Christmas, in answer to literally hundreds of prayers in his behalf, Byron walked to the pulpit in his sacrament services and delivered a message about the Savior. Never had he felt more spiritually in tune, and never had he felt such a desire to share his testimony.

As January of 1985 began, Byron again spoke, only this time at their Stake Conference. He knew that his legs had been given back to him so that he could serve, and speaking became an integral part of this service. Thus, in the months and years to come, he and Caryl spoke seventy times together, always providing hope and understanding to those who heard them.

When Byron would conclude his remarks, he felt compelled to share the following thoughts, which he titled "Happiness Is":

Happiness is being able to get yourself a drink.

Happiness is being able to brush your own teeth. If you don't think so, go home today and have someone else brush your teeth for you.

Happiness is feeding yourself. When someone else feeds you, they give you what they want to eat, not what you want to eat.

Happiness is being able to drive your car. I can drive again, but I can't get anyone to ride with me. Since I had my neck fused, I can't turn my head to check out the traffic, so I've devised a system before pulling into traffic. I count three cars, and then blend in.

Happiness is being able to hug your wife and children. I thank the Lord that I am able to do that again. He gave me a miracle, and I shall give him my life and my testimony that HE LIVES!

This was a period of increased service for Byron as he was again called to serve with the High Priest Group in his ward—this time as an assistant to the Group Leader. He was humbled with the calling and took the opportunity, whenever possible, to also teach the group lesson. For Byron, there was only one way to wear out, and that was in the service of the Lord. He had experienced so many surgeries and had so many "new parts" inserted into his body that he felt in ways like he was bionic. For this reason, he was flattered whenever his ward friends called him by the now legendary title, Bionic Bishop.

And Caryl, in spite of her physical problems, was called to serve once again. This time, in response to the request of the stake presidency, she was given the assignment of Stake Primary President. She loved children, and her experience of teaching a full load of piano students throughout her lifetime gave her the confidence necessary to proceed.

One day in late 1989, Byron's nephew, Dee Fowlks, came to his shop for a haircut. After exchanging pleasantries, Dee said, "Byron, I have to tell you how badly I feel about the tragedies you've experienced in this life. It just doesn't seem fair."

"Oh, no, Dee," Byron countered, "you just don't understand. I've had a great life, and I could never complain. I've been able to get married to the finest woman in the world. In addition, I've seen my kids grow up, go on missions, attend college, and get good jobs. Believe me, I've had a marvelous life!"

Byron's response startled Dee, and moments later, as he bid Byron farewell and headed out the door toward his car, his mind kept repeating Byron's words. Within seconds, he was seated behind the wheel, staring blankly at the small barber shop before him. As Byron's words, "I've had a great life," came again into his mind, he found himself weeping softly, grateful for the lesson on attitude and perspective that his uncle had just provided him. This moment of learning would become pivotal for Dee, an anchor and a guideline for his life.

And so, as the 1980's fell into the pages of history, Byron and Caryl entered the 1990's with renewed energy and hope. Although Byron was now cutting just a few heads of hair each day, he was still working, and so lives were impacted. Little could he believe that after forty years of life-threatening problems, he could enjoy his limited health enough to continue making a contribution to his fellow man. In Byron's mind, no man was more blessed than he.

• EIGHT •
HAWAIIAN HONEYMOON

Peace I leave with you, my peace I give unto you: not as the world giveth, give I unto you. Let not your heart be troubled, neither let it be afraid. John 14:27

One morning, prior to Christmas of 1991, Byron arrived early at his barber shop. A moment later, Ned Winder, still one of his loyal customers, arrived for his bi-monthly cut.

"Morning, Ned," Byron said, as his friend entered the room and removed his favorite Stetson hat.

"Morning, Byron. Are you and Caryl ready for Santa?"

"I'm not sure we're ever ready, Ned, but we always seem to make out. At least the grandkids think so."

"I'm not sure if mine do or not," Ned answered, chuckling. "You won't believe this, Byron, but through my "seven Winders of the world," I have thirty-four grandkids. Needless to say, with a family of fifty members, Christmas is a bit overwhelming for Gwen and me."

"Well, I want to thank you for still putting all those lights up around your house, Ned. Caryl and I drive down Winder Lane every Christmas season and thrill with the decorations you have there."

"Thanks, Byron. It's nice to know that our work is appreciated. I tell you, since I had my quadruple bypass open-heart surgery several years ago, getting that display set up is quite a chore."

"I guess we're both working on borrowed time, aren't we, Ned? It's hard for me to believe that I'm here cutting your hair, after all I've been through."

"You're just too ornery to retire, Byron, and that's great!"

"Actually, Ned, I think I would die if I quit working. But, you know, I wouldn't even be here if it wasn't for men like your uncle, George."

"How's that, Byron? I'm not sure I follow you."

"Well, just to mention one time, I'll never forget the day he came in and put one thousand dollars in my hand to help pay for a surgery I was having. My insurance had been cancelled by that time, and his kindness was an answer to prayer, believe me."

"He's always said that you were one of his best employees, Byron, and one of his strongest, too."

"Things sure change, don't they, Ned," Byron sighed, shifting his weight on his stool as he continued to cut. "But I wouldn't change my being a barber for anything."

"You haven't been a barber," Ned responded quietly, looking at Byron through the mirror.

"What do you mean, Ned? I don't want to appear proud, but I think I've been a pretty good barber, even if my customers all have to slide down in the chair so that I can reach their hair."

"Oh, you've been that, Byron, which is why I wouldn't let anyone else cut my hair. But, what I'm saying is that this hasn't been your profession. You're not a barber, Byron, you're a teacher!"

When Ned said those words, Byron felt a surge of electricity flow through his body, and he tingled with understanding born of the Spirit.

Seeing that Byron was visibly moved by what he had said, Ned continued. "The Lord knows your heart, Byron, and he gave you the gift of teaching so that you could help others. If you think of the several thousand times people have sat down to listen to what you had to say as their hair was cut, then you would know the impact you have had. I wouldn't be surprised when we pass through the veil to learn that your arthritis was nothing more than a vehicle for the Lord to use you in teaching His children what they needed to know to improve their lives. Makes sense, doesn't it?"

By now, the haircut was finished, and so, without speaking, Byron removed the cloth and motioned for Ned to arise. After exchanging the generous fee Ned insisted upon, Byron knew but one response. And so, raising his arms as best he could, he put them around his dear friend, and the two of them embraced. Each could feel the other's love, and each knew in his heart that an insight, born of the Spirit, had been shared that day.

Christmas came and went, and before Byron knew it, he and Caryl were packing their bags for the honeymoon of a lifetime! For years, they had talked of going to Hawaii and enjoying a dream vacation. Little did they expect that Caryl's second mother, LaVelle, or "Velle", would use part of her father's estate to make this trip possible for her and her brothers and sister. In all, nine people were making the trip—Velle, Jack and Dorothy Nielson, Bill and Shirley Ashburn, Richard and Kathy Nielson, and of course, Byron and Caryl.

It was January 17th, Byron's 62nd birthday. They had purchased their traveler's checks at the bank, had received final approval on Byron's eye from Doctor Call, and had eaten Byron's favorite meatball sandwich from Subway Sandwich as a birthday treat. Now they were back home and packing. Byron had visited with each of the kids and grandkids on the phone as they had called to wish him happy birthday. Little did he know that this was the last time, in mortality, that he would hear their voices and their words of love.

The next morning, although delayed by a fog inversion, they finally flew to San Diego en route to Honolulu. Several hours later they arrived on the island of Oahu and transferred immediately to Aloha Airlines. Within an hour, they landed on the island of Kauai and were shuttled to their rented condo.

Byron was given special treatment each step of the way, and he and Caryl were having the experience of a lifetime. Although it was difficult for him, he was able to walk and to ride, and he looked forward to enjoying the beautiful garden island that, years earlier, had been the filming location of the movie, "South Pacific."

The week passed too quickly, with memories being made each hour of each day. Finally, knowing that this day was their last on that paradise island, the family arose early so they could enjoy it to their fullest. After a breakfast of sausage, eggs, cereal, and toast, they left the condo. On their agenda was further sightseeing and shopping. Lunch consisted of a hamburger and onion rings, Byron's favorites, and then a trip to the beach.

When they arrived, the sun was shining brightly, and sunbathers dotted the beautiful, white sands. Some were wearing bikini bathing suits, and Byron joked, saying, "My neck hasn't turned that far in years." That was Byron, always the life of the party, seeing to it that the others had fun.

Later in the evening, Byron, Caryl, and the others enjoyed dinner at a seafood restaurant. For Byron, this meant large fried shrimp and a shrimp salad. For him, and for Caryl, this was a perfect final meal to a perfect final day in Hawaii.

That night, after they had retired to bed, Byron drew Caryl to him, resting her head on his shoulder.

"It's been quite a week, hasn't it, Little Susy," Byron stated matter-of-factly.

"One of the happiest of our lives, Byron."

Neither spoke, but each revelled in their own thoughts, re-living the events on that beautiful island paradise.

"I love you, Caryl Mackay," Byron sighed, finally breaking the silence.

"Oh, I love you, too, Byron," Caryl answered, squeezing him as she spoke. "And I have so enjoyed being able to sleep with you, even though you haven't had as much room to turn over as you've needed."

"I've had all the room I wanted, hon, and I wouldn't have it any other way."

Silently, Caryl turned and kissed her husband, grateful to be near him and to feel so spiritually as one with him. And as she did, Byron, ever the romantic, thought back to that day, nearly five decades earlier, when he first kissed Caryl Nielson, the girl of his dreams.

The trip home was uneventful, and before long Byron and Caryl found themselves driving up to their home, the same modest dwelling they had built before they were married.

After calling Peggy and Sandra to tell them of their safe return and of the good time they had, Byron invited Caryl to lie down on the sofa to watch the news on TV.

At 11:30 P.M., Byron glanced over, and saw that Caryl was fast asleep. Calling to her as he had done for what seemed like a lifetime, he said, "Caryl, we'd better go to bed."

Caryl arose to put on her nightgown while Byron excused himself and went into the bathroom. A moment later, Caryl heard his voice, a frightened voice, call her name. Rushing to the bathroom, she found he had fallen to the floor.

"What happened, Byron? Are you alright?"

"I . . . uh, just got dizzy for some reason . . . tried to make it back to my chair, but fell. Call Michael. But don't worry, I didn't hit on anything. I'm okay."

Minutes later, Mike arrived from his home through the back fence. Lifting Byron up, he assisted him over to the stool by the kitchen window. As he did, Caryl noticed that Byron was dragging his left leg, which was unable to respond. Byron then attempted to pick up his eye drops from the table, but his hand was unable to grasp the small bottle.

"You just need a good night's rest, Dad," Mike whispered.

He and Caryl then assisted Byron into the bedroom, noticing that his speech was slurred and that he was unable to make sense with his words.

Caryl then called the other children, who were almost instantly at their side. After giving Byron a priesthood blessing, Caryl called the paramedics, who came and immediately transported him to St. Mark's Hospital.

When they arrived, they immediately scanned Byron's brain, revealing that he had suffered a cerebral hemorrhage, or a stroke. The doctor on call indicated that Byron had just hours to live and that the blood flowing throughout his brain would ultimately shut down his bodily functions.

Mike called Dan in California, who was miraculously able to take the last seat on an early Sunday morning flight out of San Jose. At 9:30 in the morning, Dan walked into the hospital room and was met by Caryl and the others. Tears flowed freely, and each took their turn at Byron's side, expressing their final words of love.

EPILOGUE

Moments later, as the warming rays of sunlight streamed through the hospital room window, and with her children speaking quietly, Caryl found herself deep in thought. Emotions were somehow held back as she scribbled the final verse to a poem she had taken the previous hours to compose. It read simply:

A Tribute To My Sweetheart

> Byron was no ordinary man.
>> He was a spiritual giant—
>> A body less than perfect,
>> A life of quiet pain,
>> A soul of strength and courage.
>
> Yes, Byron was no ordinary man.
>> He raised the hopes of others,
>> He gave them love and cheer.
>> He showed them life eternal,
>> He led the way—so clear.
>
> Now, Byron is no ordinary man.
>> He follows close the Savior,
>> He lives as Jesus taught.
>> His life is now a legend,
>> With quiet miracles wrought.

Caryl Nielson Mackay
January 26, 1992

At 10:55 that morning, Byron's heart stopped. Five

minutes later he took his final breath, allowing his spirit to free itself from a body that had conquered so much for so many years.

While Byron breathed his last, little did he or the family know that at that very moment an opening prayer was being offered in his ward sacrament service, petitioning the Lord to allow Byron to be free from pain and from his earthly prison.

Meanwhile, in unison, the family gathered quietly around Byron's bed. Caryl, sitting at his side, smiled emotionally as she grasped his crippled, lifeless hand. As Lane closed the door to the room, he noticed a gold-plated sign on the back of the door. Calling Mike over to him, together they read these words:

Check-Out Time 11:00

Upon hearing these words read, Peggy said, "Dad's final, humorous thought for us. He wouldn't have wanted to pay for an extra day in the hospital."

Caryl, with tears now flowing freely down her cheeks, silently cried, Run, Byron, run! No one can physically hurt you again! I love you, darling, and I'll pray for you there, as you must pray for me! Now, flex your spirit muscles, Byron, and I'll be in your arms and kissing you before you can say "A-Rapid-Apparatus"!

Meanwhile, at Winder Dairy, several miles to the southwest, a newsletter had just been printed. In the editorial section called "Ned's Corner," Ned Winder gave a brief summary of the life of his dear friends, Byron and Caryl. In concluding his article, he had penned these words:

MY VOTE FOR VALENTINE COUPLE OF THE WORLD GOES TO BYRON AND CARYL MACKAY.

ABOUT THE AUTHOR

Born and reared in Utah, Brenton G. Yorgason served an LDS mission to Florida and Puerto Rico, and was set apart as a special missionary while stationed in the Army in Vietnam. He later received a PhD from Brigham Young University, majoring in Family Studies and minoring in Marriage and Family Therapy .

Brenton is author or co-author of over 40 books, with total sales of well over one million copies. In addition to writing, Brenton is a practicing marriage and family therapist and an owner of an auto leasing business.

Brenton and his wife, Margaret, are the parents of seven sons and two daughters, and reside in Sandy, Utah.